Victory's Journey

MOVING ON
WORKBOOK

Laverne Weber Ministries

LAVERNE WEBER

WITH HEIDI GREGORY

VICTORY'S JOURNEY MOVING ON WORKBOOK

NOTE: While the stories in this book are based on true events the details and names have been changed to protect the anonymity of those involved.

Design: 4One Ministries

Subject Headings: 1. Counseling   2. Discipleship   3. Personal Growth

ISBN: 978-0-9991966-3-2

Printed in the United States of America. All rights reserved.

What People Are Saying About Victory's Journey Moving On:

"We each have a story. When our story is connected to God's story, He can bring healing and wholeness to our brokenness. In *Victory's Journey*, Laverne Weber offers hope and practical help to those who have been hurt through the tragedy of abuse. I highly recommend this manual as a resource for all of us."

-**Bryan Koch**, *PennDel District Assemblies of God Assistant Superintendent, Senior Pastor at GT Church West Lawn, Reading, PA, founder of Brian Koch Ministries, Author, and Speaker*

"*Victory's Journey* Ministries is an excellent training course designed to help men and women deal with the emotional pain of their past. This course designed by Rev. Weber is well organized and easy to follow. While utilizing psychological principles, the material remains biblically sound.

The *Victory's Journey* Manual is a complete tool and is presented in a concise and clear manner. It offers instruction for group facilitators as well as providing a basic format for each of the group meetings. Having served as a pastor and a mental health therapist, I strongly recommend this program. "

-**Dr. David Scolforo**, *Professor: University of Valley Forge*

"People come into our churches just as they are—with wounds that have held them back from experiencing the joy of their salvation and inhibited in their ability to love and serve the Lord and others. *Victory's Journey* addresses this serious issue by providing a process for healing that we believe is critical to Christian discipleship.

We have seen men and women being released from encumbrances and freed to fulfill God's purpose for their lives."

- **Chaplain John Puleo**, *MA, Board Certified Professional Counselor*
- **Ruth Puleo**, *Women of Purpose Director, PennDel District Assemblies of God*

"We've been using *Victory's Journey* small groups for ten years and many lives have been impacted and changed by the truth of God's word and the healing process as presented in Laverne Weber's curriculum.

I was immensely relieved in 2007 when Laverne shared her curriculum with us for helping women overcome the devastatingly shameful consequences of sexual, physical and emotional abuse. I had traveled my own healing journey with the Holy Spirit and God's Word so I found it exciting to see much of the same process revealed in her original curriculum, *Journey to Joy*.

The ladies found this small group to be a safe place to process their pain, interact about what they were learning and receive help in exchanging the ashes of rejection and abuse for the beauty of a new identity in Christ.

I highly recommend *Victory's Journey* small groups."

-**Angela M. Coon**, *Author, Speaker, Blog: Hand Me Downs www.angelamcoon.com*

"For the past eight years, *Victory's Journey* has been an integral component of our ministry at Newport Assembly of God Church. The combination of Biblical truth and small group support is central to the study. We have seen dozens of women and men move from painful pasts to freedom in Christ.

But *Victory's Journey* doesn't stop there. The program also equips for the future so participants do not repeat the patterns that cause so much frustration in their lives.

I can't tell you the number of times I have heard women talking to other women and saying, "*Victory's Journey* taught me...."

I feel honored to recommend this program to anyone searching for more of Christ in their life."

 Rev. Kristen Hill, *Newport Assembly of God Women's Pastor*

"*Victory's Journey* was instrumental in my healing. The love and acceptance found in this small group ministry helped me look at my past and release the pain, shame and guilt that was defining who I was. Today I am free to move into all God has for me knowing that I am His and He is mine."

-**Pamela Wisniewski**, *Small Group Leader*

DEDICATION

To all the men and women of courage who have completed this program

and found their victory in Jesus!

ACKNOWLEDGEMENTS

I would like to thank all those who have worked so hard from the very first to help me make this manual and this ministry a reality. There are many who have contributed with their thoughts and encouragement and with editing, typing and printing the material. I would especially like to thank Heidi Gregory, Pam Wisniewski, Gretchen Duff, Tina Kester, John Puleo, and my husband, Pat.

Thank you to Jamie Holden and Adessa Holden for helping me publish this curriculum, making it available for others to use and obtain victory in their lives.

Most of all, I'd like to thank my precious Heavenly Father who birthed a seed in my heart and then fanned it into a flame. May this ministry always bring glory to His name!

. . . being confident of this, that he who began a good work in you will carry it on to completion until the day of Christ Jesus. - Philippians 1:6

VICTORY'S JOURNEY MINISTRIES

Dear Group Members,

I would like to welcome you as you begin your journey towards the joy God has prepared for you. You may have asked the question, "How do you fix a broken heart, broken dreams, a broken life? I want to encourage you that God knows your situation. He understands your pain, rejection, fear, shame and sorrow. He asks you to follow Him, to be totally His own, just as you are, even in the pains of all your past hurts.

In the middle of your everyday life, God calls you aside to hear His voice. In Isaiah 51:3 we learn that the Lord comforts and has compassion on your place of ruins. He promises to make the wasted land like the Garden of Eden, a place of joy and song. His desire, according to Song of Solomon 2:4, is to take you into the banquet hall of His presence and there pour blessings on you! Joel 2:25 is a promise of restoration for wasted years.

I am convinced that this program will lead you to find healing because of promises from God's Word like Philippians 1:6. Jesus Christ wants to complete the work He started in you at salvation. I believe in what God has said. I believe it for me and I believe it for you, dear Reader. Hold onto His promise. Be confident. Our God is faithful!

This journey will take hard work and determination but if you do your part you will see the promised hope and restoration. At times you may be tempted to give up, but in those hard times remember that others have taken this journey and made it through to the healing power of Jesus Christ. You can do it, too!

In Christ's love,

Laverne Weber

Rev. Laverne Weber

Director

CONTENTS

INTRODUCTION

"Victory's Journey" is a ministry dedicated to helping emotionally and spiritually wounded people find healing. The program is usually done as a small group healing ministry, but it can also be used individually or as discipleship training. Whatever format you choose, I would like to welcome you as you begin the journey towards the joy God has for you. It is good!

Key Verse

Being confident of this, that he who began a good work in you will carry it on to completion until the day of Christ Jesus. - Philippians 1:6

Our Purpose

Jesus Christ offers abundant life. It is God's desire to see His sons and daughters enjoy the life He gives. He wants us to be all we can be in Him. His Word has so many promises for those who follow His ways. Here are a few for you to hold on to during this journey. We suggest you write them on cards and carry them with you until they become a part of your thought patterns.

You have made known to me the paths of life; you will fill me with joy in your presence. - Acts 2:28

For I know the plans I have for you," declares the Lord, "plans to prosper you and not to harm you, plans to give you hope and a future. - Jeremiah 29:11

Motto: Look and Live

God wants us to face our pain, to look at it. It is a part of our history and ignoring it will only produce more pain. When we identify the thing that holds us back, we can really give it to Jesus.

Letting go and trusting our loving God allows us to live the abundant life Jesus promised to all His followers in John 10:10.

Group Guidelines

1. Be Honest

You will receive only as much from this group as you are willing to share of yourself. No one will insist on you telling any details that you do not wish to tell. However, as you verbalize your memories you are the one who will benefit. Remember truth sets us free.

2. Be a Confidante

Because people in this group will be sharing secrets from their past, it is essential that these things be kept within the group. It is also important that the names of members in the group be kept confidential. DO NOT even discuss these things with your spouse or closest friend (who you know will never tell). Sometimes little things might be allowed to slip and they could be very damaging to the people involved and their families.

We must each treat what is shared in the group as a gift. Act in such a way that they know they can trust you, both in the group and out of the group. Should someone in the group break this confidence, the group leaders will speak to that person privately, quite possibly asking that he/she not return.

3. Be Considerate

There will be times when one or two do most of the sharing. However, it should not always be the same one or two. If talking comes easily for you, you may need to be careful not to monopolize the conversation. If you have a hard time sharing, plan to share early in the session. You can read something you wrote.

Give others the time they need as they collect their thoughts and gather the courage to talk. Don't interrupt. Be caring and thoughtful in any remarks your do make.

4. Be Sensitive

As people share, there are times when they may need the person beside them to reach out and touch their arm or pray with them. There are other times when they do not want to be touched. It is best to let the group leaders take the first step in going to someone or praying with someone. Give words of encouragement to each other. As we each care about the others in the group, we will flow in loving support. We will also feel the Lord prompting us with thoughts we can share, and checking us when we should not speak out.

5. Be Accepting

You may have been taught not to feel a certain way, but, as memories long buried come to the surface, so do feelings. It is very important that we realize feelings are not good or bad; they just are. It is what we do with them that makes the difference. If we keep them buried they will destroy us. If we expose them, deal with them, and let God heal them, we can be set free.

As closed doors are unlocked, strong feelings will come out. As a group, we accept each person as they are with the feelings they are experiencing at the time. Since we cannot make ourselves feel differently, we need God's help. In James 5:16 we are told to *"confess our sins to each other and pray for each other so that we may be healed."* This is the essence of the group ministry.

6. Be Willing to Ask for Help

Be considerate of others, but know that you can call someone else in the group for prayer when you are having a rough time. You are not in this alone. You may need help one day, but someone else may need your help another day.

7. Be Committed

Your attendance and participation affect everyone in the group. Don't let other things, even important ones, prevent you from receiving and being a blessing.

Journaling is an avenue for releasing memories, hopes, and feelings. It's an opportunity to express ourselves without fearing anyone's opinion. It even has physical benefits, as we release the pent up emotions connected to what we are writing, we release some of the stress associated with those feelings.

Decide to memorize Scripture, and do it. The Word of God is given to us to hide in our hearts. It helps us know God and follow His plan for us. As we read the Bible, the Scriptures have a cleansing effect on our thoughts and attitudes. They bring us comfort and hope. Praying God's Word is very effective. God's Word produces godly fruit.

If you are serious about this, you will welcome both the encouraging and challenging comments from your leaders. Remember, they are concerned for you and they love you. Allow God to use them to help you grow.

8. Pray for your leaders

Victory Journey's Progression

"Victim"

⇩

1. Painful event

2. Wrong view of God, self, and others

3. Denial

4. Symptoms of a problem: fear, nightmares, anxiety attacks, anger, promiscuity, guilt, shame, addiction

5. Anger/hate

6. Reaching out for help through counseling/group

7. Beginning to share: facts, fears, anger, needs, shame

8. Acknowledgement of pain, with validation of that pain by others

9. Putting responsibility where it belongs

10. Sharing with spouse or friend (as led by the Holy Spirit)

11. Confrontation (when led by the Holy Spirit)

12. Choosing to release the past to God

13. Trading obsessive thoughts for thoughts from God's perspective

     a. Praying and praising God for Who He is

     b. Journaling or drawing

     c. Reading your Bible and meditating on it (Ex: Psalms 91 and 23)

     d. Calling your leader or a brother or sister

14. Forgiveness by choice

15. Peace, remembrance without pain or shame

16. The ability to reach out to others

17. Receiving a white stone, a symbol of winning, much like the key to the city

⇩

"Victor"

.

WEEK 1:
WHAT ARE FEELINGS?

The cheerleaders shout, the fans yell, and everyone is smiling. It's a victory! Whether it's a football game, a race, a spelling bee, or an actual war it is all about winning. A lot depends on that victory. In fact, that victory can alter the course of our futures and possibly the futures of those who come after us. Do you see yourself as a winner?

God, our loving Creator, designed a beautiful blueprint for each of us from the beginning of time. That blueprint is intended to bring us joy and fulfillment if we complete our part in the race of life. We want to be winners, but there is an enemy who wants to stop that from happening. His name is Satan, which means adversary or opponent, and he works hard to defeat God's plans. God wants us to win! His good plans are waiting for us to grab them and move forward in them. Only God knows what will happen if we dare to do just that!

> *For I know the plans I have for you," declares the Lord, "plans to prosper you and not to harm you, plans to give you hope and a future. - Jeremiah 29:11*

Take a look at the Introduction. Read the key verse and look over the purpose and motto.

Our motto is "*look and live*". What does that say to you? Does it give you hope?

The purpose of your first week's meeting is to help you look forward. A huge key to success is setting goals and staying focused on completing them. It can be beneficial to write God a letter telling Him what you hope to gain from this journey.

This will not be an easy journey. To find healing we do have to face issues and that can be hard. As you face some hard issues, you may feel anxious, discouraged, and fearful. Feel free to contact one of your leaders for prayer and direction. If you are doing this on your own, find a strong Christian who can be there when you need to talk to someone. Remember that you are already a survivor and that God will always be there for you.

The problems in your life are a big deal to God. Because He cares so much, He has led you to this place and to this time. Know that you are beginning a journey with a special group of people. As the journey continues, you will get to know a lot about each other, you will mourn and laugh together, and you will pray for one another. As God heals your hurts from the past (or present) you will be free to be all He has planned for you to be.

This journey involves dealing with areas of pain that you have not totally faced before. God, in His love, gives humans the ability to "turn off" certain areas of memory until they are able to deal with them. But if you do not deal with these feelings they will surface in other areas of life. This can result in times of uncontrollable anger or an inability to cope with seemingly small matters. You may live in a heavy fog of depression, unable to be all you feel God wants you to be, but not sure why.

Yes, you can ignore the pain or you can go back prayerfully and begin the process. James 5:16 and 1 John 1:9 speak of confession as a step towards freedom and healing. That is your part. For, as you look at your pain and share it with others who care, you can learn to walk in the freedom God has made available through the cross. God desires to give you abundant life. It is yours if you will only *"look and live!"*

No pain is too small; no pain is too big. Both can prevent us from being all God intends us to be. If you are here, your pain is significant. It is affecting your life and needs to be dealt with. Yet God has the power to work in you more than you can even imagine because it is His power that is at work (Ephesians 3:20). Invite Him to search your heart. He will lead you.

Joy is a gift of gladness that your loving Heavenly Father wants to give you in a measure so full you cannot contain all of it. This joy was bought for you with the precious blood of Jesus, God's Son. To have this gift we must be in Christ (John 17:16-26). We must receive Jesus, His gift of forgiveness from our sinfulness, and His teachings. As we allow God to be Lord of every aspect of our lives, He takes our pain and replaces it with His love, peace, and joy.

In the middle of your everyday life, God calls you aside to hear His voice. In Isaiah 51:3 we learn that the Lord comforts and has compassion on your place of ruins. He promises to make the wasted land like the Garden of Eden, a place of joy and song. His desire, according to Song of Solomon 2:4, is to take you into the banquet hall of His presence and pour blessings on you! Joel 2:25 is a promise of restoration for wasted years.

Please take time to write a prayer to God using the following scripture:

> *The LORD will surely comfort Zion and will look with compassion on all her ruins; he will make her deserts like Eden, her wastelands like the garden of the LORD. Joy and gladness will be found in her, thanksgiving and the sound of singing. - Isaiah 51:3*

Look at the following passage.

> *But now, this is what the LORD says-- he who created you, Jacob, he who formed you, Israel: "Do not fear, for I have redeemed you; I have summoned you by name; you are mine.*

> *When you pass through the waters, I will be with you; and when you pass through the rivers, they will not sweep over you. When you walk through the fire, you will not be burned; the flames will not set you ablaze. For I am the LORD, your God, the Holy One of Israel, your Savior" - Isaiah 43:1-3*

What promises do you have as you begin *Victory's Journey?*

God's Word promises us in Isaiah 43:1-3 that even though we will pass through some rivers, some waters, and some fire, God is with us. Problems and conflicts need to be dealt with, and that means going through them instead of around them. It means allowing ourselves to feel the pain so that we can release it to Jesus. The promise here is that we can come through the waters and the fire in hope and victory.

This journey will take hard work and determination, but if you do your part you will see the promised hope and restoration. At times you may be tempted to give up, but in those hard times remember that others have taken this journey and made it through to the healing power of Jesus Christ. You can do it too!

Make this verse your prayer:

> *Search me, O God, and know my heart; test me and know my anxious thoughts. See if there is any offensive way in me, and lead me in the way everlasting. - Psalm 139:23-24*

Some people say they don't have feelings. Others are very aware of their feelings. Let's talk about feelings, thoughts, and actions. What are they?

Feelings, Thoughts, and Actions

    Feelings -

    Thoughts -

    Actions -

Feelings are not good or bad, they just are. Some examples are sadness, joy, anger, fear, peace, and hope. A feeling is a sense of comfort or of discomfort.

Can you think of a feeling you have had that was positive and made you feel good?

What about one that made you feel very uncomfortable?

While feelings are just emotions, if we do not deal with negative feelings they can grow into roots of bitterness and strongholds of the enemy that will hurt us later.

Thoughts are impressions on the mind. We have a choice what we will think about. What should we think about in Philippians 4:8?

What can thoughts and meditations produce?

> *My heart grew hot within me. While I meditated, the fire burned; then I spoke with my tongue. - Psalm 39:3*

This verse states that thoughts (meditations) can ignite feelings, and in the end produce actions such as speech. We are responsible for the choices we make, even in our thought-life.

Actions are the physical or outward speech or behavior that comes from our hearts and thoughts.

> *For out of the heart come evil thoughts, murder, adultery, sexual immorality, theft, false testimony, slander. - Matthew 15:19*

Moving On

Have you ever met someone who acted on feelings alone? How comfortable were you around that person?

What is the best pattern to follow?

As we give God permission to search our hearts and know our thoughts, He will help us deal with what we need to deal with and help us to find true victory!

God began a good work in you, and you can be sure it is His intent to complete the job. That is encouraging. God is for you, and He is working with you and in you as you yield to Him. He is not mean or harsh, but He does need us to trust and obey if we are to fulfill our purpose. As we do even the worst situations can become a blessing. Why? Because of Jesus in us!

Next Week's Assignment:

1. Bring a journal. Also, decide where to keep it at home. You may start writing some early memories or thoughts about being in the group. You might want to write about any uncertainties you have.

2. Begin to memorize Philippians 1:6.

Remember, there will be times when you would rather stay home. It is important that you make the commitment to be here, regardless of how anxious you may feel. This is part of the healing process, and it will get easier.

Leaders and Group Members:

NAME	PHONE & E-MAIL ADDRESS	ADDRESS

Note: Confidentiality stands even if you should leave the group.

Prayer requests:

WEEK 2:
WHAT IS PAIN?

Did you ever smash your finger in a car door or break your big toe? I can still remember when the groomsmen kidnapped me right after my wedding. They pushed me into the back seat of a two-door car and I put my foot on the front seat (which was folded forward) to support myself. Just that quickly someone sat on that seat and as the seat back came down on my big toe there was a pop. It hurt! I not only saw stars; they danced in front of me. Now I know that no one intended to hurt me, but I had to fix the problem with a splint to allow that toe to heal. Our pains in life need a "fix".

Why is it necessary to look at past pains? Because unresolved pain leads to bigger issues. The pain in my toe isn't as severe today because I have already survived the initial incident, and healing took place. As each one of us looks at our past pain, we can find healing and abundant life. Jesus is waiting to help work through the process. You can succeed because of His great power at work in you and because of the support of those who really care.

Our key verse is Philippians 1:6, "*being confident of this, that he who began a good work in you will carry it on to completion until the day of Christ Jesus*". Read it and think about what God has done in your life to grow you and complete you. The One who began the good work in you at your salvation has many more good things in store. Try to say Philippians 1:6 by memory. How confident are you that Jesus is going to do a complete and a good work in you?

What is Pain?

Everybody carries some junk in their backpack that they really don't need. Whether big or small, that junk weighs us down and keeps us from being all that God wants us to be. You matter to God! The problems you face are a big deal to Him because He cares so much for you, even if you do not feel that way right now. In fact, He cares so much He has led you to this time and this place so that you could find healing in His love.

In dealing with the healing of past pain, we need to identify past and pain. The past is anything _____ today. It can be from your childhood or from later in your life. Pain is something that has caused you to _____. That suffering cripples you and prevents you from being all that God intended you to be.

Don't say, "My pain is too little to mention." If you are affected by it, it needs to be healed so you can move on in your life. Don't say, "My pain is too big for God to do anything." God says in Ephesians 3:20 that He *"is able to do immeasurably more than all we ask or imagine, according to his power that is at work within us."*

It is not the size of the pain, but the _____ that pain has caused in your life that matters.

Different people react differently to pain. That can be a way of coping. God gives us the ability to shut down areas of emotion and memory when we are not able to deal with the distress. There may be whole blocks of time that seem to be missing in a person's life. The person knows something is wrong but may not be sure what it is. Other people know what happened but have shut down any emotional response. After a while they find they have difficulty even feeling good feelings. Some people wear "masks". At first this helps to cope with the hurt, but in time these masks become walls to hide behind. Often hurting people just don't know how to come out into freedom. Others ignore the pains of the past.

If we deny or ignore the past pain we can end up stuck under a heavy fog of depression or anger, unable to be all we feel we were meant to be. Ignored pain does not go away. Instead, it becomes like a cooking pot on a hot fire that is not watched. The pressure keeps building until the lid pops off, leaving a mess. Pain that is not dealt with will find another way out, and it will often hurt someone else. It is so much better to go back prayerfully and be healed.

One of the first steps in the healing process is to identify the pain.

There are five types of pain. They are as follows:

1. Physical - severe illness or injury to yourself or a loved one

2. Spiritual -

      a. Disappointment – someone you looked up to failed you. Therefore you see God as failing you, and you cannot trust Him.

      b. Past or current sins (Rebellion leads to deception.)

3. Emotional – hurtful relationships and rejection

4. Negligence – abandonment, lack of proper care and provision

5. Sexual (may be subtle or suggestive) – any violation of privacy in the sexual area

Sexual abuse always produces _____ in the victim. God made us to feel pleasure when certain areas are touched. A child feels guilty for enjoying these sensations. That is a violation of the conscience. And the abuser often makes the child feel that they are to blame.

Abusers seek out vulnerable victims. Some abusers want help, but they don't know how to get it. They are afraid of losing their reputation or their friends. They need God, too.

Why do we need to look at past pain? Because pain that is unresolved leads to a variety of problems. Headaches and illnesses can result from blocked pain. Marital conflicts, even passed on abuse, are not uncommon. The spouse and children may become secondary victims.

God wants to heal you. He made you very special and He has a good plan for your life.

Look at the following verses. What key truths stand out to you?

> *For you created my inmost being; you knit me together in my mother's womb. I will praise you because I am fearfully and wonderfully made; - Psalm 139:13-14*

> *"For I know the plans I have for you," declares the Lord, "plans to prosper you and not to harm you, plans to give you hope and a future." - Jeremiah 29:11*

Satan, our enemy, wants to stop us from being the person God plans for us to be. He wants us to hurt and pass the hurt on. The choice is ours. The process of healing is not easy and it may take time, but if we are willing to start, God will be there to help us.

The journey starts as we confess our pain, our shame, and our own sins to Jesus. (1 John 1:9). He forgives us and cleanses us. Then, as we allow Him to search our hearts and open us up to His love and grace, as we share our hurts with those who truly care, and as we begin to grow in God's ways, the healing will happen!

A good prayer to remember is Psalm 139:23, *"Search me, O God, and know my heart."*

How can we be more open to God's "flashlight"?

Next Week's Assignment:

1. This week take time to think about who God is. Write your thoughts in your journal. Do the page in your workbook, "Who is God?"

2. Pray for others that are on the journey with you. Ask God to help all of you to do the assignments and journaling.

3. Take the Personal Evaluation on page 93. It's a good idea to put it in a sealed envelope and keep it for the last week.

Who is God?

Look up the following verses and see how God is described:

Jehovah-Jireh = _____Genesis 22:14

Jehovah-Rapha =_____Exodus 15:22-26

Jehovah-Tsidkenu =_____Jeremiah 33:14-16

Jehovah-Shammah =_____ Ezekiel 48:35

What does God promise in the following Scriptures?

Psalm 27:9-10 _____

John 14:16-18 _____

Hebrews 13:5 _____

What can you do when you feel God is not there for you? (see 1Chron. 28:9, Jer. 33:3, 1John 5: 14-15)

Who is God? (Look up God's characteristics in your concordance)

WEEK 3:
WHO IS GOD? - PART 1

Many of us get upset about certain things and then wonder why we react the way we do. Our reactions are frequently linked to two things – our past pain and our current expectations. It is important that each of us looks at our issues realistically if we want to be healed. It is in looking at them that they can be dealt with.

What is something that bothers you?

Why does it bother you?

Some common excuses for not dealing with issues are:

1. "It was so long ago. Why bother?" What does Hebrews 4:13 say?

2. "I can't tell God." What does Psalm 139:3 say?

3. "No one will believe me." What does Jeremiah 17:10 say?

4. "Nothing will change." What does John 8:32 say?

Many people are hurting. They say, "I'm fine" but much of who they are is affected by things they are trying to forget. Denying or minimizing is an example. It is a form of hiding. Adam and Eve hid from God and then cast blame. David covered up his adultery and murder, but it still had to be dealt with. Peter was afraid of the consequences if he admitted to being with Jesus, so he denied Him. We do not want to deny or minimize our feelings. Instead, we need to bring them into the light of God's love so we can deal with them and put them under the blood of Jesus where they can no longer destroy us. Jesus has helped you to this point, and He wants to completely heal you. He is there with you in the darkest time.

> *"Though the mountains be shaken and the hills be removed, yet my unfailing love for you will not be shaken nor my covenant of peace be removed," says the Lord, who has compassion on you.* - Isaiah 54:10

Feelings that are not dealt with will come out in other ways, such as physical symptoms, emotional disorders, or behavioral problems. Fear, moodiness, shame, relationship difficulties, vulnerability, and negative self-talk are only a few of the problems that can come from repressed pain. It is as you share your hurts that you can be all God wants you to be. In fact, there is a definite relationship between the amount of sharing and unloading a person does, and the amount of healing received. While it is painful to share, it is much more hurtful to hold in pain or shame. In the group, each person will learn to accept their feelings and those of others. Then they can learn to release the pain and be free of feelings that are destructive.

Journaling is very important. It can help you get a better understanding of why you feel the way you do. Just getting started can be tough, but remember, you can be creative in your journaling. Try writing letters to God, drawing pictures (even if they are stick figures), and making collages.

Our relationship with God, our Parent

1. Who is God?

He is the Almighty Creator, the Holy One, the King of Kings. Do you think of Him as near or far away? Think about God as a parent. Repeatedly He tells us this is who He is. How does that make you feel?

God does not equate with an earthly parent, not even a good one. The Bible pictures God for us as the perfect parent! He fathered you. He is your strong foundation and security. When He gave you birth He had a desire for you to be His child.

In Deuteronomy 32:18 God says,

> *You deserted <u>the Rock, who fathered you</u>; you forgot the God <u>who gave you birth.</u>*

In Isaiah 9:6, He is always there for you.

> *For to us a child is born, to us a son is given, and the government will be on his shoulders. And he will be called Wonderful Counselor, Mighty God, <u>Everlasting Father</u>, Prince of Peace.*

Matthew 6:8-9 tells us He cares for each of us and our needs.

> *Do not be like them, for <u>your Father knows what you need before you ask him.</u> "This, then, is how you should pray: "Our Father in heaven," (shows established relationship)*

How do we become His children?

> *You are all sons of God <u>through faith in Christ Jesus</u>, - Galatians 3:26 (NASB)*

John 1:12-13 tells us we must receive Jesus and believe in His Name:

> *Yet to all who did <u>receive him</u>, to those who <u>believed</u> in his name, he gave the right to become <u>children of God</u>-- children born not of natural descent, nor of human decision or a husband's will, but born of God.*

How do we live as God's children?

> *Therefore, brothers and sisters, we have an <u>obligation</u>--but it is not to the flesh, to live according to it. For <u>if you live according to flesh. you will die; but if by the Spirit you put to death the misdeeds of the body, you will live.</u> For those who are led by the Spirit of God are children of God. The Spirit <u>you received does not make you slaves, so that you live in fear</u> again; rather, the Spirit you received brought about your adoption to sonship. And by him we cry, "Abba, Father." <u>The Spirit himself testifies with our spirit that we are God's children.</u> Now if we are children, then we are heirs--heirs of God and co-heirs with Christ, if indeed we share in his sufferings in order that we may also share in his glory. - Romans 8:12-17*

Verse 13 says we have an obligation. This is not condemnation (Rom 8:1), but the willingness to be open to conviction because we want to please Him. To please Him we need His help. Our part is being willing to start on the path to victory.

Satan wants to use _____ to control you. Verses 15 and 16 tells us that fear is not God's will for you. He does not want you to be a slave to fear. Children do not need to live in fear of their parents.

The witness in our spirits that we are indeed God's children is given by the Holy Spirit. How does He do that?

In verse 17 we see that the life of following Jesus and being a child of God may include suffering. It is not always an easy road, but there is a promise. You are an heir of eternal life! It is not for what you can get, but because you love Him.   (Remember He first loved you.) Job really had a powerful faith in His Father God. What did he say in Job 13:15?

Next Week's Assignment:

1. Check out what God is like according to the Bible, using your concordance.

2. Keep on journaling and praying for one another.

WEEK 4:
WHO IS GOD? - PART 2

What did you learn about what the Bible says about God? Our relationship with God is based on His Word, not what we feel. While feelings are very important, truth in Jesus is what sets us free. Allow the Scriptures we look at in this group to penetrate deeply into your spirit. There is great power in absorbing and meditating on what God says to us.

My father was a great example of God's love. I knew the rules but I also knew he loved me unconditionally. My mother loved me and I knew it, but her scolding and criticism contributed to my feeling that I wasn't as good as I should be. The result was I knew God loved me unconditionally, BUT I had a hard time believing that He enjoyed me just because I was His child. 1 John 4:16-18 taught me that as I became secure in my love relationship with my Heavenly Father I could begin to expect His favor over my life. That brought so much freedom!

How we view a parent can affect how we view God. How do you view your father? … your mother? Can you see a relationship to how you view God? This might be a good time to journal on your relationship with your father or mother.

Our relationship with God, our Parent (continued)

2. How does God "parent" us?

Deuteronomy 1:31 says He _____ us.

> "… in the wilderness. There you saw how the Lord your God <u>carried you, as a father carries his son, all the way you went until you reached this place."</u>

In Isaiah 49:15 He reminds us that even if our earthly parents may _____ us, He will not:

> "Can a mother forget the baby at her breast and have no compassion on the child she has borne? Though she may forget, <u>I will not forget you!"</u>

Isaiah 66:13 tells us when we hurt, He _____ us.

> As a mother comforts her child, <u>so will I comfort you;</u>

This wonderful God also takes _____ in us. He quiets our spirit with His love, as we rest in Him. This gives us the picture of a parent rocking their child.

Zephaniah 3:17 says:

> "The Lord your God is with you, the Mighty Warrior who saves. <u>He will take great delight in you;</u> in his love he will no longer rebuke you, but will rejoice over you with singing."

He enjoys giving us good _____ according to Matthew 7:11:

> If you, then, though you are evil, know how to give good gifts to your children, how much more will <u>your Father in heaven give good gifts to those who ask him!</u>

Remember that good gifts to God are not necessarily material gifts.

In Luke 13:34 He _____ us close to Himself:

> *...how often I have longed to gather your children together, as a hen gathers her chicks under her wings, but you were not willing!*

Think how God is like a parent.

Are you allowing Him to be all He wants to be in your life? (Our lack of trust can hold back the flow of God's blessings.)

How do you feel about God being your Father?

We must be willing to put our past ideas/concepts of a parent, or father, behind us and reach toward what God's Word says He is!

Here are seven simple steps to knowing who God is according to His Word:

1. Confess the Word of God as totally true.

2. Believe on Jesus Christ and ask Him to forgive your sins. Decide to follow Jesus in all the areas of your life.

3. Praise God for who He is and what He has done, and is doing, in your life.

4. Reject Satan's lies.

5. Pray and read the Bible, and think about what it is saying to you.

6. Act on what the Word says to do.

7. Fellowship with other believers in a Bible-teaching church.

Maybe you have a handle on the fact that God loves you, but you fear His discipline. God does not want you to live in fear. After all, He loves you. But sometimes discipline is necessary to guide us in the right way. If we obey God's gentle nudges He will not have to give harder prods! If He does have to discipline us He knows what we need and is there to help us.

> *And have you completely forgotten this word of encouragement that addresses you as a father addresses his son? It says, "My son, do not make light of the Lord's discipline, and do not lose heart when he rebukes you, because the Lord disciplines those he loves, and he chastens everyone he accepts as his son."*
> *- Hebrews 12:5-6*

Remember.....

> *the Lord is good and his love endures forever; his faithfulness continues through all generations. - Psalm 100:5*

3. What is our role in the relationship?

God proved His character to the children of Israel. He made promises to Abraham and to Moses and He kept His promises. He took them out of Egypt, He led them through the wilderness, He supplied their every need, and He never left them. Israel's reaction to all this was that in every trial they cried, "I want to go back to Egypt." They were so busy complaining about what they didn't like that it seems they hardly noticed all the miracles!

What could they have focused on instead?

What is your focus?

They easily went back to their idols. They easily gave up. They forgot their God, the One who loved them, fathered them, carried them, provided for them, and would always be willing to be there for them. They even made a golden calf and worshipped it!

What idols get between us and our relationship with our Heavenly Father?

Idols can be thoughts and actions.

Joshua had been there through the long wilderness journey. Moses was dead and the responsibility of leadership into the Promised Land was his. What did God say to Joshua?

Read Joshua 1:1-9. Note the points that are underlined here:

> *After the death of Moses the servant of the Lord, the Lord said to Joshua son of Nun, Moses' aide: "Moses my servant is dead. Now then, you and all these people, get ready to cross the Jordan River into the land I am about to give to them--to the Israelites. I will give you every place where you set your foot, as I promised Moses. Your territory will extend from the desert to Lebanon, and from the great river, the Euphrates--all the Hittite country--to the Mediterranean Sea in the west. No one will be able to stand against you all the days of your life. As I was with Moses, so I will be with you; I will never leave you nor forsake you.*
>
> *"Be strong and courageous, because you will lead these people to inherit the land I swore to their ancestors to give them. Be strong and very courageous. Be careful to obey all the law my servant Moses gave you; do not turn from it to the right or to the left, that you may be successful wherever you go. Keep this Book of the Law always on your lips; meditate on it day and night, so that you may be careful to do everything written in it. Then you will be prosperous and successful. Have I not commanded you? Be strong and courageous. Do not be afraid; do not be discouraged, for the Lord your God will be with you wherever you go."- Joshua 1:1-9*

This Scripture applies to every Christian. What is your part in your relationship with God?

There were more promises from God, but ... Joshua had to do his part to receive those promises. He did and we read that God was with him as He promised.

However, as Joshua neared the end of his life there was a question that had to be settled. In the twenty-fourth chapter of Joshua we see that he assembled all the tribes to present themselves to God. Joshua reminded them of all God had done for them, and then came the ultimate decision, the big choice.

> *"Now fear the LORD and serve him with all faithfulness. Throw away the gods your ancestors worshiped beyond the Euphrates River and in Egypt, and serve the LORD. But if serving the LORD seems undesirable to you, then choose for yourselves this day whom you will serve, whether the gods your ancestors served beyond the Euphrates, or the gods of the Amorites, in whose land you are living. But as for me and my household, we will serve the LORD." - Joshua 24:14-15*

We MUST choose... each of us for ourselves. Who will you serve? Who will you follow in your thoughts, words and actions? Who will be your God? What choices can you make that will help you to heal?

Moving On

You may want to pray, addressing God as "Daddy". That is Scriptural (Romans 8:15). Practice praying to your Loving Father this week.

WEEK 5:
THE POWER OF GOD'S WORD

God's Word is very important in our lives and in our healing. The Scriptures affect us in a number of ways. Reading Scripture helps us to know what God wants us to be and do. It is powerful in purifying our minds, in healing our hurts, and in helping us to walk closer to the Lord. What are some ways God can help us through His Word?

Discuss the following verses:

> *But whenever anyone turns to the Lord, the veil is taken away. Now the Lord is the Spirit, and where the Spirit of the Lord is, there is freedom. And we all, who with unveiled faces contemplate the Lord's glory, are being transformed into his image with ever-increasing glory, which comes from the Lord, who is the Spirit. - 2 Corinthians 3:16-18*

The veil in this passage clouds our understanding. If we allow God to remove it we can see God's truths and it will be reflected in our lives. God's Word is true. It stands when other ideas and helps fail. Reading it has a cleansing effect on our thought patterns.

> *Sanctify them by the truth; your word is truth. - John 17:17*

> *…make her holy, cleansing her by … the word,- Ephesians 5:26*

Do you struggle with past guilt and shame? What tool has God given us to make us clean and even holy?

> *I have hidden your word in my heart that I might not sin against you. - Psalm 119:11*

The Word helps us defeat temptations. You do not have to be a victim!

> *The law of the Lord is perfect, refreshing the soul. The statutes of the Lord are trustworthy, making wise the simple. - Psalm 19:7*

The Word revives us and brings blessings. What character trait will you grow in if you allow the Word to revive your soul?

What are some other passages that can help you in your Christian walk?

Choose one and write it as a prayer from you to your loving Heavenly Father.

WEEK 6:
OUR NEED FOR LOVE AND APPROVAL

Have you ever felt like you didn't belong? Like you were disposable?

There have been times in my life when I didn't feel like I fit. I felt like the proverbial fish out of water! I wanted God to make a way for me to disappear…but He didn't. Instead He kept telling me that He was with me and when I walked through the fire and through the flood He would be there. And, He was.

Maybe you have felt out of place or excluded or unwanted. Maybe you've experienced rejection by someone you loved and trusted. Maybe you just don't feel loved.

As we look at Bible characters we must realize that their stories are recorded for our benefit. Sometimes we will look at women in the Bible and sometimes men. The principles of the lesson will apply to you whether you are male or female.

Read Genesis 29:15-30.

Today we are talking about a person who was unloved because of something over which she had no control. God made us in His image and we know He desires worship and that we love Him with all our heart, soul, mind and strength (Mark 12:30). We need to feel valued and loved, too. It is basic to our human nature.

What happens if that basic need is not met?

Leah was the oldest daughter of Laban but she had a physical flaw, her eyes were "weak" or "delicate". She was not a woman that men sought after. In contrast, her younger sister Rachel was stunningly beautiful and carried herself in a confidant manner. She immediately captured Jacob's heart.

But Jacob, the deceiver, was deceived. He was tricked into a marriage with Leah, a woman he did not love and did not want. But, God….

God saw Leah's broken, hurting heart. He cared and He did something. Bearing children, especially sons, was a sign of God's favor and brought great joy to a father. Leah was the first to bear a son, whom she named Reuben meaning, _____. She said that because the Lord had seen her humiliation, now her husband would love her. Did he?

Then she had another son and named him Simeon, meaning _____ because the Lord heard that she was unloved. Does God hear us when we feel alone and that no one cares? What are some ways He has shown you His care?

Leah gave birth to a third son and named him Levi, meaning _____. She longed for a relationship with her spouse. Maybe at this point, she was willing to just be friends or companions.

Then something happened in Leah. When we are feeling so alone and unwanted we can choose to feel sorry for ourselves or to do what Leah did. At the birth of her fourth son, Leah turned her focus on the Lord. She developed her own relationship with the One who would love her completely. She worshipped God despite

her circumstances. This son she named Judah, meaning _____,
and she praised the Lord. This son would be the earthly ancestor of God's beloved Son, Jesus.

She named her fifth son Issachar, meaning _____, after she bargained with her
sister in order to spend the night with Jacob, and her sixth son, Zebulun, meaning _____,
saying that the Lord had given her a gift for her husband so he would dwell with her. She also had a
daughter, Dinah.

Leah could have lived a life of bitterness. Instead, she continued to love her husband even though that love
was not returned. In fact, it seems that with each birth, her relationship with God grew. In the end Leah was
honored by being buried with Jacob as husband and wife (Genesis 49:31).

We all need love and approval. Even if you have people who love you, you have a need for God's
supernatural love. Yet, even that is a choice. Do you receive that love and live in joy and victory, knowing
who you are and whose you are? Or do you live in sadness and defeat?

What are some steps we can take to walk in God's love?

Review the Victory's Journey progression. Can you identify where you are in the journey?

Next Week's Assignment:

Make a list of the major hurts and losses in your life from your birth to the present, and to journal on times
you have felt unloved, unwanted, or unwelcome. You may want to make a time line showing some good
events as well as negative ones.

WEEK 7:
LOSS AND GRIEF

Loss is a part of life. If you haven't already experienced it you will. Grief is a natural healthy reaction to a loss or a painful event. It is the process of facing the pain and working through it into a stage of acceptance and renewed interest in life. It is a journey from sorrow to joy.

Every situation is unique. Grief is emotional, not intellectual, and it takes time and the patient understanding of people in our lives to work through it successfully. As we look at the grief process, remember, each grief is significant, and each person is unique in the way that they deal with their pain. As Christians, we have hope that things will get better as we put our faith in the Lord Jesus Christ.

What are some situations that produce a sense of loss?

We usually associate grief with death, but this is not the only loss we need to face. When we lose someone we love we feel loss. When someone abuses a child, they steal something from that child. It might be innocence, trust, or self-worth. Adults can be abused, too. We must allow ourselves to grieve these losses or we will be like a volcano ready to erupt either towards ourselves or others, maybe even towards God.

Read the following Scriptures about God's comfort:

Psalm 30:5, 11-12; Isaiah 61:1-3; Psalm 23; and Revelation 3:20

God is faithful and He is always there even when we are not aware of His presence. He wants to come into our hurt and bring hope.

Defining grief and the grief process

Grief is the process of _____ through the pain into a stage of acceptance and renewed interest in life.

    A. Grief is the normal, _____ response to loss.

    B. The grief process is the journey of working through the pain or the loss.

        1. There are various stages.

        2. It involves _____ and _____.

        3. It is unique to each individual.

        4. It is very emotional and often painful.

Stages of the grief process

A. Shock

B. Isolation

C. Denial

D. Anger

E. Fear

F. Guilt and severe pain – it is important that you allow yourself to feel but not to stay there. Do something healthy to release the pain.

G. Bargaining

H. Depression, anger turned inward. Friends may wonder why you aren't "better".

I. Acceptance

    1. Understanding

    2. Forgiveness of person(s) who caused loss

    3. Letting go of the pain, wanting to feel happy again. There may be some guilt connected to this. Remember your Heavenly Father rejoices over you; He wants you to do that too. Try short joy-trips where you do something just for fun and you choose to smile.

    4. Restoration of hope in the future, normal functioning, and the ability to think of the future in a realistic way.

Things that help

A. Writing, music, art, scrapbooking

B. Living memorials such as planting a tree, donating Bibles through the Gideons

Remember, the Valley of Grief is just a phase of the journey between the past and the joy God has in store for His children who ask Him for it. You matter to God! He grieves when you grieve. Isaiah 53:4 says Jesus carried our griefs. Any pain is too big for us to carry alone. Don't be stuck in a prison of pain. Let the Lord take your burden. Reach forward for your healing.

Next Week's Assignment:

Do the following paper on "My Loss…My Feelings", then write in the journal about your losses and how you feel about each one.

My Loss…My Feelings

Draw a picture about your loss and how you feel. Stick figures are okay

Write God a note telling Him about your drawing:

What do you need to release to the Lord?

Write out a Scripture verse that you can hold onto as you let go of this pain:

WEEK 8:
WHAT DOES YOUR PAST LOOK LIKE?

Mike had a tough history. His father was heavily into drugs and had a major anger issue. His mother was an alcoholic. After his sister was murdered, the children were taken out of the home. In the foster system, he faced abuse and incredible loneliness. He longed to be a part of a loving family.

Mike did not want his past to define who he was or where he was headed and, yet, he kept struggling with the issues of his family. He wasn't alone!

Joseph was a man of faith who believed in a God he did not see and in a dream that looked impossible. How do you view yourself? Do you see yourself as a failure, a big nobody, or as chosen by God with a purpose to fulfill?

Read Hebrews 11:1-3 and 22.

It is true that we are sinners, lacking in righteousness, and failing at godliness.

> *As it is written: "There is no one righteous, not even one"- Romans 3:10*

BUT GOD…sent Jesus to change that. As we embrace Christ's death in our stead, accepting His love and forgiveness, we are made _____ (in right standing with God). Have you accepted God's gift of forgiveness through the death and resurrection of Jesus Christ?

As we receive Christ, God takes our human bodies and puts His Spirit into us. And He gives us purpose. We can then start living a powerful, fruitful life.

But us…too often we agree with the enemy in renouncing our value instead of renouncing his lies. Satan comes to steal…to rob…to destroy. Jesus came to bring abundant life, a life of value and fulfillment.

> *The thief comes only in order to steal and kill and destroy. I came that they may have and enjoy life, and have it in abundance (to the full, till it overflows). - John 10:10 (AMP)*

How does the thief steal from us?

He _____ us. He uses our family tree, our past, our failures to make us so lacking in power and in right standing with God that we just don't….

What could you possibly achieve if you really believed God had a plan and a purpose for your life?

Joseph had a history:

Noah ➡ Shem ➡ Nahor ➡ Terah ➡ Abram, Nahor, Haran, and Sarai

(she had a different mother than Abram)

Abraham	Sarah	Nahor	Milcah
Isaac	Rebekah ←	Bethuel	????
		Laban	????

Jacob	Rachel

Joseph

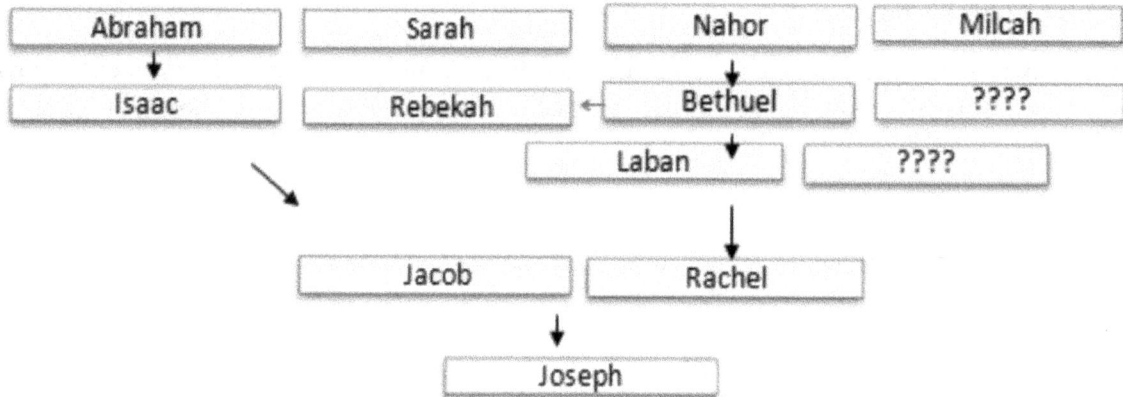

Draw a picture of your family tree:

Joseph's family:

On one hand Joseph had a not-so-godly heritage:

1. Noah – drunk

2. Abraham – lied about his wife

3. Sarah – impatient, abusive (with Hagar)

4. Isaac – lacked discernment

5. Rebekah – lied, favored one son, deceived her husband

6. Jacob – lied, cheated, manipulated

7. Rachel – disgraced because she was barren, jealous, stole, lied, deceived her father

On the other hand he had a godly heritage:

1. Noah – found grace in the eyes of the Lord, was used to bring salvation to humanity

2. Abraham – friend of God, man of righteousness and faith

3. Sarah – full of faith, mother of nations, fruitful in old age, beautiful, blessed

4. Isaac – godly man

5. Rebekah – beautiful, willing to follow God's plan, brave

6. Jacob – man who wrestled with God and won, his 12 sons became the 12 tribes of Israel

7. Rachel – weeping, beautiful, her barrenness turned to blessing

Joseph had a history – we all do.

He had an ancestry of imperfect people who _____ _____.

The Bible tells us true stories of real people. It shows us where they failed, but it also shows us how they followed God. The encouraging word is that regardless of the family history we carry we are chosen by God, and He has a purpose for us from the time of conception. That plan is not about our comfort or our worldly success. It is about the Kingdom. As followers of Jesus we belong to the Kingdom where He is King. In a kingdom the king is boss. In this Kingdom, Jesus is Master and Lord.

Yet it is a Kingdom where the King loves us. That is beyond human comprehension…not power control because He already has all power. Not greed because He already owns it all. Not recognition because all of creation sings His praises. He simply loves us and wants each of us to love Him back with that same unconditional love…that is the part that catches us. We get so caught up in "life" that we lose our passion and love for Jesus. Unconditional Jesus love will make us do unusual things. Unconditional love will make us pursue God's purpose for us over the "normal life".

> *The word of the Lord came to me, saying, "Before I formed you in the womb I knew you, before you were born I set you apart" - Jeremiah 1:4, 5*

We are so used to thinking we are the way we are and that is it! But Psalm 139 speaks of God having a blueprint that covers every part of His plan for our lives. In the secret place where we were formed He took great delight in drawing up our unique blueprint. He created us with the gifts and talents needed to fulfill His plan for us. He puts into our DNA the abilities and desires to accomplish the very blueprint He has for our lives.

It is God's desire to complete the work He began in us. (Phil. 1:6)

Read Genesis 37:1-4:

> *Jacob lived in the land where his father had stayed, the land of Canaan. This is the account of Jacob's family line. Joseph, a young man of seventeen, was tending the flocks with his brothers, the sons of Bilhah and the sons of Zilpah, his father's wives, and he brought their father a bad report about them. Now Israel loved Joseph more than any of his other sons, because he had been born to him in his old age; and he made an ornate robe for him. When his brothers saw that their father loved him more than any of them, they hated him and could not speak a kind word to him.*

The robe was a symbol of possible transfer of authority. Was this a wise move on Jacob's part? Why, or why not?

Then Joseph had several dreams (Genesis 37:5-11) and he told his brothers and then his father. What were their reactions (verses 8 and 11)?

How can we tell the difference between a God-given dream or vision and something from our own imagination or mindset?

God knows your destiny and He wants you to know it so you can take steps in the right direction. Faith believes a promise it doesn't see. Do you dare to believe?

God is not as concerned about your past heritage as you are. The Bible is filled with stories of people who did great things for God. Many of them had troubled pasts. It is to the glory of God when we grow and fulfill God's purpose for us despite our family heritage or our own personal past. God is about what you are doing now to prepare for your eternal inheritance.

Don't miss out by holding back, but go forward and become victorious!

Next Week's Assignment:

1. Journal on past family or personal background situations that hold you back from being all you could be. You could do your own family tree.

2. Fill in the "Inventory of Sins and Weaknesses" and then read Ephesians, chapters 4-6.

Inventory of Sins and Weaknesses

(Mark current issues, past issues, and generational issues. Be honest.)

Sin/Weakness	Current	Past	Generational
Pride			
Rebellion			
Self-pity			
Worldly values			
Bitterness			
Malice or evil speaking			
Disregard for God's rules (such as keeping the Sabbath, honoring those in authority, having no other "gods")			
Ingratitude			
Lying			
Pornography			
Stealing			
Devil worship			
Laziness			
Procrastination			
Immoral thoughts and/or actions (lust)			
Addictions			
Envy/jealousy			
Fear			
Depression & despair (with or without suicidal thoughts)			
Negative thinking			
Hypocrisy			

Write a prayer confessing the sins and weaknesses you marked. Renounce the effect they have had on you and your family. Ask Jesus to make you clean.

WEEK 9:
SECRETS TO DEFEATING SINS

Helen could not speak English when she started school. It was a big school with crowded conditions. Because of her language deficit, her teachers decided she was not smart enough to be in a regular classroom so they moved her to a classroom of children with mental and social disabilities. They told her parents that she could not understand the basic things of life. That is why when the only doll she ever had was taken away and given to her sister, her family thought it was okay.

This little girl grew up thinking she was unable to function. When she seemed normal her mother told her her mental illness would show itself when she reached puberty. She married and had children, and all the time, she waited. She just knew one day she would wake up, and her life would fall apart...

Until she went through the *"Victory's Journey"* program and realized she was smart and pretty and fully functional! It was a life-changer. She could rewrite the rest of her life!

Think about how you see yourself. Was this always the way you felt?

Much of how we act is based on who we think we are. If someone told you you will never be smart enough to do a certain thing you will probably act like you are not smart enough.

Look at the *"Inventory of Sins and Weaknesses"* that you filled out. What did you learn by doing this paper? Did you notice any familial trends?

Do you have some negative feelings about yourself? What are they?

Can you pinpoint when you started feeling that way? What words or situation might have started that self-view? It would be a good idea to do some journaling about this.

Negative feelings definitely influence how we behave, but sometimes we have sin that we need to confront and deal with. We need God's help to have a victorious life.

To defeat sin and overcome evil, we must put on the armor of God and use the powerful offensive weapon mentioned in Ephesians 6. What is that?

Why do you think it is called the Sword of the Spirit? Read Hebrews 4:12.

Moving On

How can we use God's Word on our own thinking patterns?

Paul writes that we should have the mind of _____ in Philippians 2:5. That is our goal. We need to replace wrong thinking and behavior with godly thinking and behavior. It is not enough to renounce personal and generational sin. We must fill our hearts with Jesus. As Paul wrote to the Christians in the Ephesian church, the Holy Spirit is also talking to us.

Read and write Ephesians 4:21-24 as a prayer.

2 Corinthians 10:3-5

Steps to Defeating Sin

1. Identify problem areas

    A. Generational issues – passed down weaknesses, attitudes and behaviors such as depression, anger, martyr attitudes, insecurity, fear, bitterness, pride, lust, , control, etc. – Exodus 20:3-6

    B. Blind spots – problems you have but do not see in yourself. It may be the very thing that really bothers you about someone else. Denying a problem prevents God from making you everything He wants you to be.

        1. Ask a spouse or close friend to help you see areas you are blind to.

        2. Observe the way people respond to you at different times.

        3. Ask yourself if your actions bring glory to God.

        4. Identify your motives when you feel upset.

    C. Strongholds – areas of frequent temptations that are so strong they result in feelings of failure, hopelessness, lust, and defeat. Victories do not last. These may be generational or may be the result of giving Satan a foothold.

        1. Were you honest on your personal inventory paper?

        2. Look up each item you checked in your concordance and read ALL the verses listed. It may take a while! Get God's perspective on the sin and allow that to change your perspective.

2. Referring to your inventory of sins and weaknesses, fill out the grid "Defeating Sin's Power In My Life"

A. Confess these carnal weaknesses, strongholds, and blind spots as sins that God hates.

B. Renounce the sins that have hindered you.

C. Ask Jesus to forgive you and cleanse you from these sins.

D. Thank Jesus that you are clean. When Satan tries to trip you remind him of the blood of Jesus that covers you. Quote a Scripture at him. (Ex. I John 1:9)

E. Have a specific goal, prayer, and Scripture for each area.

F. Walk in the light, refusing to allow your mind to go back to even consider the old thoughts.

G. Fill the empty places with good Christlike attitudes and actions. Do good for others whether you feel like it or not. Pray for those who have hurt you.

Defeating Sin's Power in My Life

Sin(s) to put off	Christlike traits to put on	Prayer	Scripture(s)

Moving On

Put off the old attitudes and actions and put on the new man (attitudes and actions of Jesus) according to Ephesians 4:22-27, 29-32 …

> … put off your old self, which is being corrupted by its deceitful desires; to be made new in the attitude of your minds; and to put on the new self, created to be like God in true righteousness and holiness.
> Therefore each of you must put off falsehood and speak truthfully to his neighbor, for we are all members of one body. "In your anger do not sin": Do not let the sun go down while you are still angry, and do not give the devil a foothold.
> 29 Do not let any unwholesome talk come out of your mouths, but only what is helpful for building others up according to their needs, that it may benefit those who listen. And do not grieve the Holy Spirit of God, with whom you were sealed for the day of redemption. Get rid of all bitterness, rage and anger, brawling and slander, along with every form of malice. Be kind and compassionate to one another, forgiving each other, just as in Christ God forgave you.

Give no place to the devil. Read Romans 13:11-14, Ephesians 5:1-21 and Colossians 3:1-15. Notice that we do the "putting off" and "putting on". It is our responsibility to actively start working towards our goal.

Pray and renounce any sin or generational problem you realized. If you are a part of a group, let your leaders pray over you.

3. **Believe that God is on your side.** You have renounced your sins. You have asked His forgiveness. You are chosen by God to be His own beloved child. You are pure in His sight! Read Ephesians 1:3-8, and comment on what it means to you.

4. **Commit yourself to living a life of service to Jesus Christ, that He might be honored in every thought, word, and action.**

5. **Expect His guidance as He takes you into new dimensions of personal worship and service.** Step out in faith, a little at a time. Don't let fear or past failures determine your future!

6. **Expect His favor on your efforts to please Him.** (Be sensitive to His leading through others.)

7. **Pray the prayer of Jabez in 1 Chronicles 4:10 daily:**

> Jabez cried out to the God of Israel, "Oh, that you would bless me and enlarge my territory! Let your hand be with me, and keep me from harm so that I will be free from pain." And God granted his request.

Next Week's Assignment:

1. Fill in the chart on "Defeating Sin's Power in my Life" with a personal prayer and a Scripture for each sin. It is good to memorize these Scriptures or write them on a paper to keep handy. That way they can be quoted to the enemy when he tries to tempt or discourage

2. Fill out the paper "From Child to Adult" and journal on how you respond.

3. Read the book of Philippians. Then reread Chapter One, writing down some key thoughts and impressions. What you write down may minister to someone else.

4. Make Psalm 139:23 your daily prayer this week.

From Child to Adult

A. Put checks by the reactions you had as a child. Double check the reactions you still have.

    1. Blamed self (guilt feelings)

    2. Blamed others - maybe even God

    3. Feelings of never "being good enough"

    4. Need to hurt or punish self

    5. Need to hurt or punish others

    6. Denial

    7. Acted as a follower without responsibility

    8. Physical "sickness"

    9. Tried to do better

    10.Tried to be strong, the "adult"

B. Check the traits you think are important. Initial the traits you have now.

    1. Independence

    2. Creativity

    3. Loyalty

    4. Perseverance

    5. Kindness

    6. Honesty

    7. Poise and confidence

    8. Problem solving skills

    9. Patience

    10.Faith

C. List two negative reactions you wish to change:

D. List two positives you have that you wish to grow in:

Now, choose a single area and ask God to help you change. Look up 3 verses that show how God can help you in that area. Read 1 Corinthians 13:11. Journal on how you will do that.

WEEK 10:
OUR CONFIDENCE

Do you trust God? Think about it. Trust may come easily for you if promises that were made to you were kept but, for many, that isn't the case. Hannah was told that if she was really good she would get to have a friend over for a sleepover and so she was! In fact, she did extra chores and worked as hard as a ten year old ever could. But the promise was not kept. That happened again and again. Hannah stopped expecting good results. Her heart grew hard, her grades plummeted and so did every other aspect of her life.

Disappointments lead to disillusionment and disillusionment leads to utter defeat. Why try to be good if it doesn't make a difference? Why even care?! People may fail us...and they often do. Those hurts leave scars and we become very skilled at turning off real feelings. Being vulnerable is out of the question!

But the Bible teaches us that God is good (Psalm 100:5). Good people act good. They do good things. Therefore, if God is good we can believe He acts good. He wants to bless us and do what is good for us. How much do you think God has for you if you will dare to be vulnerable and let Him into the scarred places?

Discuss the following verses from Philippians 1:

In verse 2, who gives us grace and peace?

Is it difficult to think of God giving good gifts?

We have looked at what God's Word says about God as our Parent. Are you starting to see a difference in the way you view Him now?

Read 2 Corinthians 1:3. How does this verse describe God?

In verses 3-5 of Philippians, how did Paul pray for the believers at Philippi?

Joy is not dependent on our circumstances for as we read through this letter we learn that Paul is writing from a jail cell.

Verse 6 is the key verse for the *"Victory's Journey"* program. What does it say to you?

Isn't it good to know that Jesus, your Good Shepherd, wants a complete healing in your life, and He will patiently do what is necessary to accomplish it.

Rewrite this verse as a prayer of thanksgiving to your Loving Heavenly Father.

Moving On

What feelings do you pick up from Paul in verses 7-8?

Read verse 9. List the three key ingredients of a successful group?

1. _____

2. _____

3. _____

Love, knowledge, and depth of insight help us bond and trust one another. The more we know others the more we love and trust them…that's true of God, too.

In verse 11 of Philippians one, who is the Source of righteousness?

Does this mean we will have an easy life as we live for Jesus? Look at verses 12 to 26. Note Paul's attitude in various difficult situations.

God's purpose is greater than ours. What seemed to be a negative in Paul's life helped others open up and share their faith more freely. We can be that person who helps someone else just by being open.

God's plans for you are good. He asks us to be good and to act in a good way. Other people's actions do not need to determine our behavior. We are responsible for what we do now.

Notice some of the admonitions Paul gives these Christians in verses 27 to 30. Pick one that applies to you.

Review the paper, "From Child to Adult". How did you feel as you wrote in your journal? Share something you wrote with your group or with someone you trust.

Next Week's Assignment:

1. Draw a picture of your family.

2. Memorize a verse that speaks to you from "My Value in Christ", and then write in your journal about it. Answer the question, "How does that make me feel?"

3. Reread Philippians 2:1-13 and write some thoughts the Holy Spirit makes real to you.

My Value in Christ

In Matthew I am

- 5:14 - light to the world

In John I am

- 1:12 - God's child
- 15:15 - Christ's friend
- 15:16 - chosen to bear fruit

In Romans I am

- 6:18 - a slave of righteousness
- 8:14-17 – a child of God and a joint heir with Christ

In 1 Corinthians I am

- 3:16; 6:19 – a dwelling place for the Spirit of God
- 12:27 – a member of Christ's Body

In 2 Corinthians I am

- 5:17 - a new creation
- 5:18, 19 – reconciled to God and able to pass that on

In Ephesians I am

- 1:1 – a saint
- 2:10 – God's workmanship
- 2:6, 19 – a citizen of God's Kingdom
- 4:24 - righteous and holy

In Colossians I am

- 3:3 – hidden in Christ
- 3:12 – chosen, holy, and dearly loved

In 1 Peter I am

- 2:9, 10 – chosen, part of God's royal priesthood, God's own possession

In 1 John I am

- 3:1, 2 – a child of God who will resemble Christ when He comes for His Church
- 5:18 – born of God and the evil one (Satan) cannot touch me

WEEK 11:
WHO AM I?

Read Philippians 2:1-13:

In Philippians 2:1 we have a great encouragement in being one with Christ. Take time to consider the wonderful position that places us in as Christians. It is easier to deal with past hurts when one knows one is in a positive meaningful relationship with the King of Kings.

Love provides comfort. You are loved! Allow yourself to feel Christ's love and comfort. His love took Him to Gethsemane and Calvary. Think about His rejection, His death, His shame, His grief, and that He did it for you so you would not have to carry those burdens. There is fellowship with the Holy Spirit, the third Person of the Trinity, Who walks alongside the believer. We are not alone anymore.

In verses 2-4 we see that the life of love and service requires us to be one in _____ and _____. What characteristics should we adopt and what things should we avoid if we are to be like Christ?

In verses 5-11 note the attitude of Christ. Do an attitude check. What were the positive effects of Christ's attitude in verses 9 through 11?

Verses 12-13 tell us that God has a purpose. We need to let Him lead us to its completion.

Hebrews 12:1-2 tells us to cast off our weights. Then healing can be expected.

What regrets do you have?

What stresses you? What fears or insecurities hold you back from being totally free in Christ?

Journal on the weights you need to release to Jesus.

Review *"My Value in Christ"*. Name some principles of truth that we must accept and hold on to, such as the fact that we are forgiven through Jesus Christ. We must each choose what we will believe, the Bible or Satan's lies. Valuing yourself means thanking God for making you and then caring for yourself. We are children of worth.

Next Week's Assignment:

1. Write in your journal about a fear or insecurity and do the papers on "Regret or Self Contempt" and "Dealing With Guilt".

2. Read Philippians 2:14-30 and journal on positive and negative relationships you are in now. How do you think your childhood relationships set the patterns for these relationships?

Moving On

"Dealing with Guilt" is based on David's prayer to the Lord after his sin. His cry is one of desperation but also one of faith in who God is. God so loved us that He gave us His one and only Son. His love is a forever love.

Remember what He says to us in 1 John 1:9.

> *But if we confess our sins to him, he is faithful and just to forgive us our sins and to cleanse us from all wickedness. (NLT)*

Regret or Self-contempt

God's Forgiveness

If we confess our sins, he is faithful and just and will forgive us our sins and purify us from all unrighteousness. - 1 John 1:9

After God's Forgiveness

Regret - accepting that forgiveness but wishing it had not happened, knowing it cannot be undone, awareness of broken pieces of life, confidence that God uses broken pieces to make something beautiful…

or

Self-contempt – feeling that "I have failed in a certain area" means "I am a failure" and "I will always be a failure", the inability to move beyond self-hate, the inability to see newness in Christ, choosing to receive Satan's accusations as truth.

How I View Myself   How God Wants Me to View Myself

_____

_____

_____

_____

What is the truth?

What will I choose to do with this truth?

What is my future hope based on this truth?

Dealing with Guilt

Unfounded guilt is blame the enemy or other people put on you, often for things they have done. Stepping into freedom only happens when we can identify our feelings of guilt and then decide if they are false guilt feelings or real guilt feelings. If they are false guilt feelings we must give them to Christ and refuse to take them back. This takes choosing to speak only truth to ourselves.

Name any guilt feelings you have and decide if they are false or true. Have you already asked God to forgive you?

True guilt is something that God will forgive you of if you ask Him. Read Psalm 51 and answer the following questions:

1. What are your sins? (verse 3)

2. Who do we really sin against when we sin? (verse 4)

3. What does the psalmist rely on when he asks for forgiveness? (verses 1,6,14)

4. What sacrifice pleases God? (verse 17)

5. What hope can we have? (verses 7-12)

6. What is our responsibility after we are forgiven and restored? (verses 13-15)

Other Scriptures to read are as follows: Ezra 9:5-7, Nehemiah 1:5-7, Psalm 32:5, Psalm 38:4-18,

Acts 19:18, Hebrews 10:19-22, James 5:16, and 1 John 1:9. (Write out one of these Scriptures that ministered to you.)

Journal: Write a prayer of thanksgiving to God for removing your guilt. If He has removed it what right do you have to bring it back up? Memorize your prayer and use it against the enemy when he tries to remind you of your past.

WEEK 12:
TRUTH OR LIES?

What do you believe is true about yourself?

What is a godly self-concept?

Read Mark 4:35-41:

> *That day when evening came, he said to his disciples, "Let us go over to the other side."*
>
> *Leaving the crowd behind, they took him along, just as he was, in the boat. There were also other boats with him. A furious squall came up, and the waves broke over the boat, so that it was nearly swamped. Jesus was in the stern, sleeping on a cushion. The disciples woke him and said to him, "Teacher, <u>don't you care</u> if we drown?"*
>
> *He got up, rebuked the wind and said to the waves, "Quiet! Be still!" Then the wind died down and it was completely calm.*
>
> *He said to his disciples, "Why are you so afraid? Do you still have no faith?"*
>
> *They were terrified and asked each other, "Who is this? Even the wind and the waves obey him!"*

Did Jesus care?

Why were they terrified after the wind died down and the seas were calm?

Read Romans 8:28 & 29

> *And we know that in all things God works for the good of those who love him, who have been called according to his purpose. [29] For those God foreknew he also predestined to be conformed to the image of his Son, that he might be the firstborn among many brothers and sisters.*

How do these verses make you feel?

Next Week's Assignment:

1. Read Philippians 3 and journal.

2. Do the papers "Response to Anger" and "Anger's Actions".

3. Journal on a good result that came from one of your past pains.

Response to Anger

1. What triggers my anger?

2. Do I always react the same way when I am angry or when I feel one of my "rights" is threatened?

3. Is my perception of the situation true? Do I know all the facts? Do I know both sides?

4. Have I asked God to let me know the truth?

5. Could there be a different way of looking at this?

6. Am I at fault?

7. Have I prayed for the other person(s) involved?

8. Do I feel God's love towards the other person(s) involved? Can I accept this person as he (or she) is and as loved by my loving heavenly Father?

9. Do I love him (or her) and God enough to do what it takes to heal the division? (ie. Ask forgiveness for my part?)

10. Am I willing to release my feelings and "rights" to the Lord and let them go?

11. Is my heart's prayer, "Lord, change me"?

    A. Make me more humble like Jesus in Phil. 2.

    B. Develop certain character qualities (or fruit) or spiritual gifts in me.

    C. Correct me and change my ways through God's loving discipline.

    D. Prepare me for greater responsibility or leadership.

12. Do I believe the Holy Spirit will help me?

Anger's Actions

Briefly describe a time when you felt angry (or frustrated or irritated) this past week:

Check the way you express your anger:

__loud voice	__harsh words	__slander
__drugs or alcohol	__foolish behavior	__malice (meanness)
__glaring eyes	__wrong dress	__strife, division
__verbal abuse	__avoidance	__profanity
__stealing	__vandalism	__rape
__pornography	__clenched teeth	__lying
__worry	__blaming	__depression
__abuse	__arguing	__fretting
__irritability	__lack of appreciation	__fear
__door slamming	__over-sleeping	__lack of patience
__silent treatment	__denial	__abnormal eating

Who is usually the target of your anger?

When did you start using these "anger actions"?

Pick a verse in Psalm 31 to use as a prayer and pray it each night and morning to the Lord

WEEK 13:
FREEDOM FROM ANGER

Have you ever felt that your faith had become a little frayed? When we are struggling with difficult issues we can easily lose our focus on the Lord.

Read Philippians 3:1. What is a key that Paul gives us to guard our faith?

James tells us that faith without works is dead (James 2:17). Works are good but they do not get us into God's Kingdom.

In Philippians 3:2-7, what attitude should we have towards relying on our good works for God's grace?

Sometimes we also hold on to hurts and fears. How does holding on to such things make us feel?

Is it hard to give up our attitudes towards our past achievements or our past mistreatments?

Verses 8-11 are a powerful statement of what is important in our relationship with Jesus Christ. What is our goal?

Why does God allow certain things to happen?

People make choices. Our free will allows us to do that. Is God responsible when we make bad choices? Or when others choose to hurt us?

Consider Christ's righteousness. How do individuals achieve righteousness?

What purposes might God have in allowing people to suffer pain?

What purposes might He have in your situation?

As Paul talks about striving towards knowing Jesus and being able to share in the resurrection from the dead, he stresses the value of faith. Suffering may be a part of our lives. Maybe you have suffered and you don't understand why. Read verses 1, 8, and 10 again. Summarize what they tell us.

Read Philippians 3: 12-16.

The past may be filled with good things or difficult things. We must look at the past, deal with it, and then be willing to put it behind us before we can truly move forward into God's plan.

Review Philippians 1:6.

Moving On

Our goal is to win the prize of eternal life. How are we to strive towards that goal?

In Philippians 3:17 to 4:1 Paul tells the Philippians to imitate him and others who follow him. How can you do that?

Is Jesus able to transform hurt individuals? What is our part in the first verse of chapter 4?

As we consider our past and the choices we have about how we will deal with it, we need to take a look at anger. Anger is just an emotion but if not handled properly, it will be destructive to others and to us.

Anger occurs when we feel that our rights have been violated. Little children often "stuff" their anger to cope with the pain. That is not healthy.

Steps to Freedom from Anger

Moses was God's man, but when he saw an Egyptian beating an Israelite he reacted. His emotions took over, and he killed the Egyptian. As a result of his anger he was forced to leave all he knew and flee to a distant desert.

Anger in itself is just an _____ or feeling, neither good nor bad. It is what we do with it that can destroy us and others. That is sin and sin produces bondage. The more we give in to any bondage the more powerful it becomes. Angry people will say hurtful things, try to control the lives of others, be verbally and physically abusive, act impulsively, and cause tension in their environments. Unchecked anger often prevents people from living effective Christian lives. Attempting to control the anger leads to more and more stress.

Anger takes two primary forms: overt hostility towards others or passive anger turned inward, which can turn into depression. Both forms steal life and joy. God's Word holds the key to victorious living!

It is important that you understand the difference between depression and normal grief. It is normal to grieve over losses. Refer to the lesson on "*Grief and the Grief Process*".

The key to freedom from anger is to want to change. These are vital steps in helping you find that freedom:

1. Identify the _____.

2. Get the _____!

3. Accept personal _____. (Ephesians 4:31, 32; Colossians 3:8)

4. See your anger through the _____ of those you are hurting.

5. Use your anger as an _____ to deal with the real issue.

6. Act _____ to recall and correct past offenses.

7. Regain _____ areas from the enemy (Satan) – see Ephesians 6:12.

    a. Confess the sin that caused the anger.
    b. Claim the power of the blood of Jesus.
    c. Ask God to take back any area you have allowed Satan a stronghold in.
    d. Submit that area of your life 100% to God.
    e. Memorize and quote Scripture when the enemy attacks you.

8. Forgive your _____ – be willing to carry their pain – see Matthew 18:21-35.

9. Find the _____ from the events that caused you to react.

10. Give God all your _____ _____.

11. Be _____.

12. Be _____ with the Holy Spirit.

> *Be angry, and do not sin; ponder in your own hearts on your beds, and be silent. Selah (Pause and think about that.) -Psalm 4:4 (ESV)*

Next Week's Assignment:

1. Read Philippians 4. Write how verse 3 applies to your group.

2. Begin to memorize a meaningful verse from Philippians 4 or another one from "My Value in Christ".

3. Write in your journal why you chose the above verse and what you need God to help you with.

WEEK 14:
CARING FOR ONE ANOTHER

God created Adam, and He said, *"It is not good for man to be alone."* That is the only time during creation that God said something was not good. We humans are different from animals in that we are created in the likeness of God Himself and deep within us there is a void that cries for relationship. We need a relationship with God to have abundant life, but we also need relationships with other humans. Yet sometimes good relationships turn sour. Can you think of some reasons good friendships fall apart?

In Philippians 4:2-3 we read about two godly women who loved the Lord and worked hard in ministry. We don't know what the disagreement was about, but it was big enough for Paul to address it. Conflict affects the whole body and can be very hurtful.

What does Paul ask these Christian women to do?

What does he ask the church leader to do?

Notice the lack of harshness. Helping each other work through issues is part of the benefits of being part of a body of believers.

Read Philippians 4:4-9.

Compare verse 4 to Philippians 3:1, Ephesians 5:19, 20 and Psalm 50:23 (NIV). Why is this principle of rejoicing so important?

Philippians 4:6-9 lists some truths that can help us deal with fears and panic attacks. What is our role in attaining peace of mind?

In verse 10, what are some practical ways we can care for others?

In Philippians 4:11-18, what secret has Paul learned?

What does the word "contentment" mean to you?

In verse 13, we can see that this ability to be content in every situation is related to Paul's relationship with Christ, the Source of all strength.

The Philippians had served God well by ministering to Paul's needs whenever they had a chance. Because of their compassion put into _____, Paul was blessed and able to continue in ministry.

Moving On

What do our gifts become when we help those who serve God?

What gifts do you have that God might need you to share with someone in need?

Verses 19-23 of this chapter close the letter with praise, encouragement and victory! All your needs means all your needs. Christ is and has all we need! We are to live every part of our lives for His glory and it is His grace in our spirits that enables us to be victorious!

Next Week's Assignment:

Read 2 Corinthians 3:17-18 and write your thoughts in your journal.

WEEK 15:
PAIN AND SHAME

Read II Samuel 13 quietly. What feelings does this story bring out for you?

Because sin was rampant we can assume that children of both genders were abused in many ways. In our day sexual abuse is a major problem. This type of wounding will usually manifest itself in later years by behaviors that reflect anger, shame, rejection, and a need to control others. It is not only a horrific act, but one that can alter the course of a life.

Note Tamar's beauty and innocence. Was she guilty? Why, or why not?

What could she have done differently?

Was this a set-up?

Considering that Amnon was her older brother and the heir apparent, should she have felt a sense of danger?

What type of love did Amnon have for Tamar?

What counsel did he listen to?

What were his feelings after the rape?

How did Tamar respond? Note that she did not hide her disgrace.

How does this story affect your feelings about hurtful situations you could not control?

How did Absalom respond?

How did David respond?

How would Tamar have felt about that?

Why didn't her father do anything? See II Samuel, chapters 11 and 12.

This led to more tragedy. See II Samuel 13:28 and 29, and 18:33.

How do victims feel towards those who did not defend them?

God gives us accounts in the Bible to help us deal with our feelings. What principles can we learn from this story? These might include confronting the abuser with truth even if they do not receive it, releasing the pain, going to someone we trust who can help us, and leaving the place of pain. In reading God's Word, and in sharing our pain, we grow in freedom and, therefore, healing.

How did this story in II Samuel 13 make you feel? This Biblical account may be difficult if you have been a victim of sexual assault. Remember, you were the victim. Now it is time to confront your abuse. Facing your feelings is painful, but it leads to healing. Journaling allows you to understand your own reactions better.

Next Week's Assignment:

1. Journal on how the story of Tamar made you feel. Facing feelings and allowing oneself to actually feel the pain is very hard, but it is a key factor in the healing process. One idea is to write a fictional, but fact-based, story of your own abuse. You can draw a picture and journal on it as in week 7.

2. Read the first three chapters of Nehemiah. It's a good idea to memorize Galatians 6:2.

WEEK 16:
REBUILDING THE RUINS

Have you ever felt overwhelmed; that you had too many broken issues?

Nehemiah heard of the desolation in Jerusalem, and it broke his heart. He lost his joy. There are just too many Christians surrounded by ruins, broken walls, broken dreams. When we focus on all of these negatives we become discouraged. Satan's lies start to sound true, and we feel our faith and joy seeping away. We can end up living an existence that falls short of the abundant life Jesus died to give us.

Read Nehemiah 1:1-3. Nehemiah needed to know what his countrymen were dealing with. In these verses we see people living among the ruins of a past glory. They could remember the good life, but all they could see was rubble. The enemy controlled their minds with shame and put-downs. They had no protection.

Look at Nehemiah 1:

RUINS are those things that are the result of horrible pain in the past. These survivors were living in distress and reproach among old ruins. Sometimes victims even feel guilt over their "ruins". Some may be in denial about their past. The first step is to recognize a problem.

What ruins do you see in your life? Take some time to label your pains. Bring them out into the light of truth. Allow Jesus' love and the acceptance of others in the group or someone else you trust to encourage you to face each issue. Then you can begin to "look and live".

STRONGHOLDS are areas where Satan has established control. We are forgiven sinners growing in God. Sometimes we make mistakes. Sometimes we sin. In such cases we ask Jesus to forgive us, and He does (see 1 John 1:9). However, if there are areas that we cannot seem to get the victory over it may be we are dealing with a foothold (Ephesians 4:27) or a stronghold (2 Corinthians 10:4).

Review the paper on *"Defeating Sins"*. If you are struggling in an area, go back to where Satan got his foot in the door of your thoughts. Think about how that sin hurts you and the people you love. Renounce the sin and its effects. Then pray and order the enemy to leave and stay out in Jesus' Name.

WALLS represent ways that we hide. Do you have walls, or certain behaviors you hide behind?

What do you do when your defenses are gone?

Remember, these people were former exiles. They and their fathers had suffered greatly. After many decades they had returned to their land, their royal city, and a new life of hope.

However, this was a place without walls for the enemy had broken them down. Their defenses were gone. They were totally vulnerable to those around them who wanted to see them destroyed. In this case rebuilding the walls represents strength and protection, not that which keeps out healthy relationships. Why hadn't the exiles rebuilt the ruined walls?

What did Nehemiah do in verses 4-11?

This was not an easy prayer. It was not a comfortable prayer. Nehemiah was broken, and he went to the only One who could do anything about it. There are several elements in his prayer that we can learn from.

Nehemiah began by <u>recognizing</u> who God is. He worshipped God because God is powerful and mighty but also loving and full of mercy towards those who obey Him.

Then he <u>confessed</u> that the Israelites, and he and his family, had sinned terribly against God. But he also <u>reminded</u> God of God's promises to restore His people that repented and obeyed Him.

He finished with a <u>plea</u> for God to hear and give him favor with the king of Persia.

What a great pattern for us as we seek the Lord's help! He is all powerful, yet, all loving. On that basis we can confess our past sins, remind God of His promises, and ask for His favor as we continue to grow in His freedom.

Look at the second chapter of Nehemiah. Nehemiah won the king's favor because he already had the Heavenly King's favor. He went to Jerusalem, and, in verse thirteen, he surveyed the damage. He did that with just a few trusted men. What a great example!

Take an honest look at your damaged areas, then start rebuilding with God's help and that of your brothers (or sisters) in the Lord.

Verse fourteen mentions a part of the wall that Nehemiah couldn't get through on his trip around the damaged walls. Sometimes a part may be too badly damaged to deal with right away. Let God direct you to the part to deal with first.

Hope was spoken and the people chose to move with what God wanted to do. In Nehemiah, chapter 3, the people each did their share, working together for the benefit of all. That is "group"! We need other people to help us rebuild.

Discuss Biblical principles for friendship. Look up Proverbs 17:17; 16:28; 27:6, 10; Luke 11:8; Romans 15:1; Ephesians 4:2; and Colossians 3:13.

> *Bear (endure, carry) one another's burdens and troublesome moral faults, and in this way fulfill and observe perfectly the law of Christ (the Messiah) and complete what is lacking [in your obedience to it. - Galatians 6:2 (AMPC)*

Think about possible walls in your life. Are they good walls that help you establish boundaries, or are they walls to hide behind?

Next Week's Assignment:

1. Read the rest of Nehemiah. Come next week prepared to share one truth from the book of Nehemiah that you can apply to your situation. Journal on that truth.

2. From Nehemiah, chapter four, write down some principles that will help you defeat opposition and discouragement.

3. Memorize Galatians 6:2.

4. What was the result of Nehemiah's perseverance in verse sixteen of chapter six?

5. Journal on past pains that were identified today.

WEEK 17:
DEALING WITH NEGATIVE WORDS

Your family and friends may be very supportive of your journey to healing. If that is the case you are most fortunate. At other times family and friends will mock changes they see you trying to make, deny events from your past, and try to come against your efforts to receive healing. Why do you think they might do that?

Satan will try to condemn you. The difference between Satan and God is that Satan condemns us and pours shame and feelings of failure on us. God through the work of the Holy Spirit convicts us to bring us close to Himself. Remember, Jesus brings life (John 3:16-21).

We need to understand that we must always be ready to deal with spiritual opposition. See Ephesians 6:10-20. How strongly do you want to see your healing become a reality?

Look at the fourth chapter of Nehemiah. Some mocked Nehemiah and tried to block his success. Why did they do this?

According to verse 6, what do you need to do to be successful?

Set your entire spirit towards the process. It takes focus with a purpose.

Nehemiah and his men sought God. Pray and be alert to prepare yourself for possible ploys of Satan. Some people will not even recognize they are being used by the enemy to discourage you. Put on the whole armor of God Paul writes about in Ephesians 6. Our weapons are the Word of God and prayer.

Discouragement came to the leaders when they looked at the whole problem. It was just too much! Focus on one issue at a time. Let others you trust help you. And, remember that your healing affects others. It's worth working for. We gain spiritual support from each other.

In Nehemiah 6:16, the work was completed. God was glorified and future generations reaped the benefits. The final outcome in Nehemiah 8:10 was joy as God gave them His strength. He will do the same for each person who asks Him.

Are other people affected by your pain?

What are your goals?

What steps do you need to take to move forward?

What is at stake?

Next Week's Assignment:

6. Journal on your goals and what steps you will have to take to reach them.

7. Journal on any remaining issues you may have been avoiding.

8. Read the Word!

WEEK 18:
HEALTHY CONFRONTATION

The Merriam-Webster Dictionary defines confrontation as *"a face to face meeting; the clashing of forces or ideas; or comparison"*. In Victory's Journey we use the term, *"compassionately confrontational"*. Jesus was confrontational. He challenged people from where they were to follow Him into a new life. Even though at times Jesus was very strong, He loved people! He had compassion.

To most of us the word confrontation is not a pleasant one. What does it mean to you?

Think about a confrontation you had in the past. How did it turn out?

What are some principles to keep in mind when you feel you need to confront someone?

    1. Know the _____.

    2. Know _____ and your _____.

    3. Know the other _____.

    4. Use _____ words.

    5. Seek a good solution that will help everyone.

Have you ever heard of a daughter named Noah?

The story of Noah and her sisters is in Numbers 26:33 and 27:1-7. Here we see an example of positive confrontation. Note who the girls' father was. They had no rights because of their father's sin. Yet, they chose to confront those who were in authority that could help them. Do you think that took a lot of courage in that day?

In this case confrontation is not a bad word, for they came with a good attitude. God honored them. It seems they had some idea of God's grace and justice.

Think of some positive and some negative ways to confront others.

Nehemiah confronted the king, but he did it in a humble non-aggressive manner. Esther is a good example of preparing for the confrontation with prayer and seeking God. Notice her attitude of respect and the wisdom in which she set the stage for her confrontation. She did her part, and God made some other things "just seem to happen". Victory was the end result.

Next Week's Assignment:

1. Journal on people and situations which have hurt you. Write letters to those who caused the pain, using healthy confrontational approaches. In the letter(s) state what happened and how it made you feel. Delegate the blame to the appropriate person. If you are guilty for any of it, confess that. Recognize that the one behind it all was Satan. Put these letters aside. You will complete them next week.

NOTE: <u>Do not send the letters at this time!</u> These letters should only be delivered after praying about it with your leaders and as the Holy Spirit leads. Even if they are never read by the hurtful party, there is healing in the writing and the praying over them. Some people may want to read them in group, give them to the leaders, burn them, or just put them away in their Bibles.

2. Start a praise journal of thank you messages to God for things, people, Scriptures, and situations that have helped you.

WEEK 19:
FORGIVENESS

In the past, your ability to make good choices may have been affected by things like distrust, shame, anger, fear, and self-pity. As we grow in Christ it is crucial that we learn how to make the right choices.

Read Psalm 124:6 & 7 and Psalm 91:3.

> *Praise be to the LORD, who has not let us be torn by their teeth. We have escaped like a bird out of the fowler's snare; the snare has been broken, and we have escaped. - Psalm 124:6-7*

> *Surely he will save you from the fowler's snare and from the deadly pestilence. - Psalm 91:3*

What snare does God want to help us escape from?

We make a choice when we face our fears and anger and any other issues we may be dealing with. Trusting God completely is difficult if you have trusted people that have hurt you. It is good to remember our lessons on God. He is faithful and trustworthy. He loves us unconditionally. While that does not mean He gives us everything we ask for when we want it, it does mean He gives us what we need when we need it. Stepping away from the snares of the enemy means stepping into the Truth of God's Word. It means choosing to listen to the positive thoughts and words in life. It means rejecting the lies and negative concepts that Satan wants us to believe.

It also means choosing to forgive. While forgiveness is a process that God has to help us work through, we must begin by an act of our will. We must decide to forgive. Forgiveness is not a denial of the pain. It does not mean trusting. It does mean not living in the hurt. When we forgive someone we erase the list of their sins against us, and we free them to receive Christ's forgiveness. Trust, on the other hand, must be earned. It may take time to rebuild. As we grow the Lord will give us more wisdom in our trusting. Hurts are a part of life, but God can help you forgive. (That does not mean you will never be hurt again, although, as you heal, you will be less vulnerable to those who are looking for someone to hurt.)

Write down the name(s) of anyone you know you need to forgive.

Jesus tells us that if we want to be forgiven we must forgive others. He never asks us to do the impossible, so that means He will help us. God loves you and has brought you to this place of healing. It is the enemy, Satan, who was behind all of the destruction, and he is the one we fight against. The joyful truth is that in fighting Satan, we are victorious through Christ.

> *For though we walk (live) in the flesh, we are not carrying on our warfare according to the flesh and using mere human weapons. For the weapons of our warfare are not physical [weapons of flesh and blood], but they are mighty before God for the overthrow and destruction of strongholds, [Inasmuch as we] refute arguments and theories and reasonings and every proud and lofty thing that sets itself up against the [true] knowledge of God; and we lead every thought and purpose away captive into the obedience of Christ (the Messiah, the Anointed One)... - 2 Corinthians 10:3-5 (AMPC)*

Moving On

And that is just what we must do. We must each decide to put every negative thought in a box and throw it into the deepest part of the Sea of God's Forgetfulness, and ours. We must deny any proud and false thoughts access into our thinking. Instead, we must fill our minds and hearts with worship to our wonderful Bridegroom, Jesus Christ, who loves us unconditionally. Let us choose to think and speak in a positive way. Let us choose not to swim in shame and pain but to soar on wings as eagles. Read Philippians 4:8 and I Corinthians 13, especially verses 4 to 8.

God can also help you to leave behind your hurts and move into the blessings and the life He has planned for you. (Read Jeremiah 29:11.) So many people say they want to be free of the past, but they still want to carry around suitcases filled with negative thinking, bitter attitudes, and hurtful behavior. Just remember, we also have God's joy and strength to help us to deal with our hurts.

Read Deuteronomy 28:1-13 and 30:19-20 and name the blessings God wants to give His people. You might want to underline them in your Bible.

What does God want us to choose?

What have you been choosing?

Review who you are in Christ (see Week 10). What gifts and personality traits has God given you?

How can you use them to bless others?

Next Week's Assignment:

1. Write God a letter, giving Him your memories, pain, shame, anger, walls, and vulnerability. (Note 1 Peter 5:7.) Renounce their effect on you.

2. Pray, asking God to help you release your past pains to Him. Ask Him to help you receive God's love and the love and acceptance of godly people.

3. Take out the letters you wrote last week. Write letters to anyone else you still need to forgive. Tell them how they hurt you, how that felt, and how it has affected you. At the end of each letter tell them that Jesus has forgiven you, and you are choosing to forgive them. Please do not send these letters until you and your leaders have prayed over them. If it would do more damage to send them you should destroy them. Your purpose is healing, not revenge.

4. Journal about your future hopes and dreams. Replace "self-talk" with "Word-talk". Choose life!

5. Read Luke 11:21-23, Romans 8 and 12 and Ephesians 4:1 – 5:21.

WEEK 20:
HEALTHY RELATIONSHIPS

Healthy relationships don't just happen; they take work. Fill in the chart below. Luke 11:21-23, Romans 8 & 12, and Ephesians 4:1-5:21 are passages that teach us godly character traits. (Remember, we can only make choices for ourselves, not others.)

THINGS THAT DESTROY	THINGS THAT BUILD

In learning how to be all we can be, we need to understand the root causes of why we react the way we do. Draw a chart of this progression of negative reactions. You may have some other things you can add.

- Rejection, either real or perceived, leads to hurt feelings.

- When we are hurt we feel like a failure and may develop a crushed spirit.

- That crushed spirit can lead to self-pity, if we allow it.

- From self-pity, resentment towards the person who we feel caused our pain blossoms into resistance and arguing, even with other people.

- Our resentment causes us to keep records of the wrongs done to us. Unreal expectations lead to anger when these expectations are not met.

- Unresolved pain and anger pushes us to react to anything that triggers those old feelings, even if we do not recognize the similarity.

- Eventually, we isolate ourselves from God and others.

You can make your chart personal by writing in specific situations.

Moving On

Many people allow God to heal them from past issues only to fall into Satan's snare with a current relationship issue. Our enemy desires nothing more than to put us back into bondage. The principles we learn in this program are not meant to just help with the old issues; they are tools that will help with new issues as well. Learn them well and make them a part of how you handle life.

Developing healthy relational habits takes time and conscious effort. The wonderful truth is that as we do our part God will do His. One point to remember is that this life has its thorns. Thorns are not bad things. Rather, they are a means of growth to those who will learn by them. We may fail and others may fail us but if we follow the characteristics to healthy relationships we will win.

Next Week's Assignment:

1. Journal on any remaining areas of difficulty.

2. List some areas that you can work on to develop good relationship habits.

WEEK 21:
CHANGE

In most cases change is good and everyone is glad for it, but it can carry a price tag. Some people that you have been close to in the past may not like the "new" changes and may actually sabotage your efforts to become all God wants you to be. Some family members and friends may want you to continue to be weak and vulnerable, or they may want you to keep the old "masks" and not rock the boat. A few spouses will be uncomfortable with the changes in your devotion and dependence on Christ Jesus. Some may feel left out or unsure of how they fit into the picture now.

What are some situations you see in your own life?

Jesus said that we must take up our cross and follow Him. Read Matthew 10:29-39 and notice:

1. Your value – verses 29-31

2. Your responsibility before God and its effect – verses 32-33

3. Possible reactions from people who are not God-seekers – verses 34-36

4. The love-priority – verse 37-38

5. The reward – verse 39

Does this mean we brush our loved ones off and fail to love and minister to them?

Read 1 Peter 3:1-16. We have a responsibility to live in our Christian freedom in such a way that others will want what we have. Then we know we have done our best with God's help, and the choice becomes theirs. The Holy Spirit helps us do this, for in ourselves we are weak. In fact, we are just getting used to this life of freedom and joy!

What are some practical things we can do to help difficult situations?

If those you have been close to refuse to support you, you may need to back off. That does not mean that you destroy any bridges to them. It does mean you must be sure that you are putting Jesus first.

Most of all, remember that God loves our loved ones more than we do. We have wonderful promises in God's Word to hold onto. Consider these as you pray for your loved ones:

Do not be anxious about anything, but in every situation, by prayer and petition, with thanksgiving, present your requests to God. And the peace of God, which transcends all understanding, will guard your hearts and your minds in Christ Jesus.

Finally, brothers, whatever is true, whatever is noble, whatever is right, whatever is pure, whatever is lovely, whatever is admirable--if anything is excellent or praiseworthy--think about such things......... And the God of peace will be with you. - Philippians 4:6-9

Nothing will be impossible for you. - Matthew 17:20

WEEK 22:
BOUNDARIES

Pray Galatians 5:1:

> *It is for freedom that Christ has set us free. Stand firm, then, and do not let yourselves be burdened again by a yoke of slavery.*

Boundaries are good. Without them our world and our lives would be total chaos. Let's look at God as the One who knows the value of boundaries.

> *Who shut up the sea behind doors when it burst forth from the womb, when I made the clouds its garment and wrapped it in thick darkness, when I fixed limits for it and set its doors and bars in place, when I said, 'This far you may come and no farther; here is where your proud waves halt"?- Job 38:8-11*

What is the key thought in this passage?

God is not a God of confusion but of order. He ordained boundaries in nature. Without those limits we would have constant upheaval; with them we have beauty.

What do the following passages tell us?

> *When the Most High gave the nations their inheritance, when he divided all mankind, he set up boundaries for the peoples according to the number of the sons of Israel. - Deuteronomy 32:8*

> *From one man he made all the nations, that they should inhabit the whole earth; and he marked out their appointed times in history and the boundaries of their lands. - Acts 17:26*

> *A person's days are determined; you have decreed the number of his months and have set limits he cannot exceed. - Job 14:5*

> *The boundary lines have fallen for me in pleasant places; surely I have a delightful inheritance. - Psalm 16:6*

God has set boundaries for nature, nations, and for human beings. Boundaries have to do with a divine plan and purpose. It is His desire to bless us and to help us fulfill all the purpose He has ordained for us. David said that God's personal boundaries for him were pleasant.

Looking at all of these Scriptures we can agree with what Mordecai told Queen Esther in Esther 4:14.

> *"For if you remain silent at this time, relief and deliverance for the Jews will arise from another place, but you and your father's family will perish. And who knows but that you have come to royal position for such a time as this?" - Esther 4:14*

How might that be true of your life?

We looked at Joshua's promises and choices in the beginning of our journey together. Let's reread Joshua 1:1-9.

Moving On

God gave Joshua a specific calling to lead His people into the Promised Land. He established the boundaries of the area that belonged to the Israelites, but Joshua and the people had to claim those boundaries by walking them out.

What does God want to do in your life along these lines? Is there a "land" you need to take possession of? (It could be an area where you are still struggling, a relationship, or a promise for your future.)

With Joshua's call came promises. What were these promises in verses 3, 5, 7 and 8?

How can you "walk out" the promises God has given you?

The ultimate promise of success was based on God's _____ being with Joshua. God also promised that along that journey no one would be able to stand against him and his God-given authority.

There were also some things Joshua had to do. What were they in verses 6-9?

What actions must you take to receive God's Promises.

How courageous are you when you meet opposition or temptation? What can you do to improve your courage level?

People who have been hurt by other people struggle with healthy boundaries. They may make the boundaries around them like walls so people cannot get too close. Usually these people try to control their environment and the people with whom they have relationships because then they feel safe. In so doing they intrude on the boundaries of others.

On the other hand, they may not have any protective walls. In that case they are so anxious to please that they lose their identity and their God-given purpose.

Read Romans 12:2. Are we to change our personal identity to please other people?

Healthy personal boundaries happen when you know who you are, and you treat yourself and others with respect. You know you are created by God with unique qualities that are good and that He loves you. (Knowing He loves you as you are helps you love others as they are.) Remember love is not a lack of boundaries.

God wants us to feel free to say "yes" or "no" without guilt, anger, or fear. Having Christ's mindset will help us know when to say "yes" and when to say "no". It will also release you from false guilt or guilt another person is trying to put on you.

What are some practical ways you can set boundaries in your life?

One way to deal with those who step on your boundaries is take time to think about the situation. Use the time to figure out how you really feel and how to express it. Write your thoughts down on paper. Then do it. It won't be easy, but you'll feel free and strong (and a little guilty at first) – and it will get easier. Always ask, "What would Jesus do!" He set positive boundaries and He loved at the same time. We can follow His example.

Another area is to set boundaries against the enemy's temptations and attacks. Because you have been given authority in Christ (Ephesians 1:19-21) you can determine what areas are off limits to Satan. Of course, you must stand your ground after that decision has been made!

Next Week's Assignment:

1. Journal on areas where you struggle to maintain safe and godly boundaries.

2. Make a list of things you can do to stand firmly in your freedom.

Do not be anxious about anything, but in every situation, by prayer and petition, with thanksgiving, present your requests to God. And the peace of God, which transcends all understanding, will guard your hearts and your minds in Christ Jesus - Philippians 4:6-7

No onc can take your joy unless you let them!

WEEK 23:
COMPLETE SURRENDER

This has been quite a journey as we have looked at a variety of people in the Bible and examined our own similar issues. It is my prayer that you have seen victory in a number of areas as you have released these areas to God. God is going to complete the work in you as you continually give Him permission to do so.

There is a final major key to unlocking the door of freedom spiritually and emotionally. That key is complete surrender to the Savior who carried our sin and pain, and who now sits on the right hand of the Father making intercession for us.

Read Luke 7:36-50 and think about how you might feel if you'd been the uninvited guest at this special dinner party given in Christ's honor. The guests included the rich and famous in town.

Whose home was Jesus in?

What kind of a woman entered the room?

What was the reaction?

How did she react to the people who were discussing her sins?

Because her focus was completely on Jesus she was not pulled down by the voices and looks of those around her. She was intentional!

Many people who have found freedom in Christ are still seeking approval from a person who seems important to them. If that is our focus we will miss the great thrill of pouring our love on Jesus and receiving His love and approval. The others judged her as a sinner. Was it because her very presence there reminded them of their own failures?

Some Pharisees were believers. Can Christians have the wrong attitudes?

How should we respond to those who attack us?

> *My dear brothers and sisters, take note of this: Everyone should be quick to listen, slow to speak and slow to become angry,- James 1:19*
>
> *A gentle answer turns away wrath, but a harsh word stirs up anger. - Proverbs 15:1*

This woman had a shameful past. Jesus asked, "Do you see this woman?" Do you see her? Are you like this woman? Notice her tears, her love, and her extravagant service. Notice the Lord's response to her. Do you believe Jesus responds to you with approval?

What do you need to change in your mindset to have such surrender?

Moving On

She comes, knowing that the One Who matters will not condemn her. She brings her all, trusting Him completely with her most precious item. She gives Him all that she has left of herself that is undefiled. Do you see the richness of that? She did not give Him the leftovers, the dirty parts, the thing that was easy to release. She gave her most valued possession, her only valued possession, and she gave it in a way that she could not take it back. She became radical in her devotion. She broke the alabaster box!

People often hold back from giving Jesus everything because of fear. But, remember, He is not going to make worse decisions for you than you would make even if you could see from His divine perspective. He loved this woman with all her faults and He received her gift. Not only that, He gave her the gift of forgiveness. She died to herself that day at His feet in front of all of the judgmental witnesses, but she stood up in newness of life.

What was this woman's key to freedom?

She came in total humility and extreme love. She traded the old for the new. She expressed her love for Jesus with a personal sacrifice, a broken alabaster box pouring out expensive myrrh, a symbol of death. Jesus loved her with His sacrifice, a broken body, pouring out His precious blood, a symbol of life. It is interesting that when she walked away she still carried the fragrance in her hair. Jesus always gives us something beautiful when we give Him that which costs us much.

Christ calls us. He offers His gifts of life, freedom, and worth. But it isn't a one-time experience; it is a daily walking with Him in His approval until we do not even hear the voices that would tear us down. It is keeping focused on our love-relationship with our precious Lord!

That is how Philippians 1:6 works! Jesus completes the work in us as we stay close to Him because we love Him.

Pray and give whatever you are holding onto to Jesus Christ in a time of total release and surrender to His Lordship. Total surrender involves total release of our belongings, our reputation, our family, ourselves.

WEEK 24:
VICTORY!

This would be a great time to celebrate what God has done in your life. Completing this program does not mean you will never face difficult situations again. It does mean that you have tools to be victorious.

Do the repeat "Personal Evaluation". Then open the one you did at the beginning of the program and compare your answers. What do you notice that is different?

Share a testimony with your group or someone you trust.

Journaling is a good habit to continue.

God promises great things for those who overcome. One promise is that we will be given a white stone with a new name written on it (Revelation 2:17). You are a special overcomer and you can be proud of the hard work you have done. God has great things ahead and with your new mindset you can move forward in God's favor. Remember, God is still at work, and He will continue to help complete His purpose for you until the day He calls you to Himself.

Go forward in victory! This is not the end; it is the beginning of a new life!

Our next gathering will be on _____ at _____.

Please write on.....................

1. What changes have I experienced since I started "Victory's Journey"?

2. What special memories do I have from the group?

3. Where am I on the "Victory's Journey Progression"?

4. What fears do I still need to work through?

5. Where am I spiritually?

6. What are my hopes and future plans?

Please write on.....................

Personal Evaluation #1

Place a check next to any of these symptoms that you are experiencing:

☐ 1. You exaggerate, brag, or name-drop.

☐ 2. You are afraid to try new things for fear you will fail.

☐ 3. You adapt your opinions to others so they will like you.

☐ 4. You rely on addictive/compulsive behavior to numb your emotional pain.

☐ 5. You have a hard time making yourself be around people because you feel intimidated.

☐ 6. Your private self is different from your public self.

☐ 7. You frequently feel depressed.

☐ 8. You blame yourself when someone hurts you.

☐ 9. You frequently make excuses for those who mistreat you.

☐ 10. You act differently than you really are.

☐ 11. You try to solve the problems of others while neglecting your own life.

☐ 12. You are critical, focusing on the failures of others.

☐ 13. You like to dress, act, or behave in ways that are socially unacceptable.

☐ 14. You mostly spend time with people on an extreme end of the social ladder.

☐ 15. You back away from relationships with people you admire before they get to know you.

☐ 16. You make unreal demands on yourself.

☐ 17. You feel lonely.

☐ 18. You are a perfectionist.

☐ 19. You feel people would not like you if they knew the real you.

☐ 20. You sometimes feel suicidal.

☐ 21. It is hard to ask for help because you feel admitting your need shows everyone your inadequacy.

☐ 22. You resist setting personal goals.

Choose 3 or 4 of the most prevalent characteristics you checked and give a recent example for each. God heals what we expose to Him. (1 John 1:9)

Personal Evaluation #2

Place a check next to any of these symptoms that you are experiencing:

☐1. You exaggerate, brag, or name-drop.

☐2. You are afraid to try new things for fear you will fail.

☐3. You adapt your opinions to others so they will like you.

☐4. You rely on addictive/compulsive behavior to numb your emotional pain.

☐5. You have a hard time making yourself be around people because you feel intimidated.

☐6. Your private self is different from your public self.

☐7. You frequently feel depressed.

☐8. You blame yourself when someone hurts you.

☐9. You frequently make excuses for those who mistreat you.

☐10. You act differently than you really are.

☐11. You try to solve the problems of others while neglecting your own life.

☐12. You are critical, focusing on the failures of others.

☐13. You like to dress, act, or behave in ways that are socially unacceptable.

☐14. You mostly spend time with people on an extreme end of the social ladder.

☐15. You back away from relationships with people you admire before they get to know you.

☐16. You make unreal demands on yourself.

☐17. You feel lonely.

☐18. You are a perfectionist.

☐19. You feel people would not like you if they knew the real you.

☐20. You sometimes feel suicidal.

☐21. It is hard to ask for help because you feel admitting your need shows everyone your inadequacy.

☐22. You resist setting personal goals.

Choose 3 or 4 of the most prevalent characteristics you checked and give a recent example for each. God heals what we expose to Him. (1 John 1:9)

References and Recommended Reading

Seamands, David A., (1985). *Healing of Memories.* Wheaton, IL: Victor Books

Dobbins, Richard D., (1982). *Your Spiritual and Emotional Power.* Old Tappan, NJ: Fleming H. Revell Company

Frank, Jan, (1987). *A Door of Hope.* San Bernardino, CA: Here's Life Publishers.

Meyer, Joyce, (1995). *Battlefield of the Mind.* Tulsa, OK: Harrison House

Anderson, Neil T., (1990). *Victory Over the Darkness.* Ventura, CA: Regal Books

Kendall, R.T., (2002). *Total Forgiveness.* Lake Mary, FL: Charisma House.

Clinton, Dr. Tim, (2006). *Turn Your Life Around.* New York, NY: Faith Words - Hatchette Book Group USA.

Hart, Archibald D., (2001). *Unmasking Male Depression.* W Publishing Group (A Division of Thomas Nelson, Inc.).

Hegstrom, Paul, (2004). *Angry Men And the Women Who Love Them.* Kansas City, MO: Beacon Hill Press of Kansas City.

Hegstrom, Paul, (2006). *Broken Children, Grown Up Pain.* Kansas City, MO: Beacon Hill Press of Kansas City.

Comments and Answers for Workbook

(Please try to answer these before looking below.)

Week 1: What are Feelings?

Page 15 – Our motto is "Look and Live". To live the abundant life we must be willing to look at our past in the light of God's truth. Then we must release our pains to Jesus and step into His wonderful life.

Page 17, 18 –
Feelings – a sense of comfort or discomfort
Thoughts – impressions on the mind
Actions – Physical or overt speech or behavior

The best pattern to follow is:
Feelings – Thoughts – Action (F-T-A)

Week 2: What is Pain?

Page 21 – Fill in the blanks:
- Before
- Suffer
- Reactions

Page 22 – Fill in the blank:
- Guilt

God created us with a good plan and a good purpose. Praising Him for what He has done will open our hearts so we can receive healing.

Week 3: Who is God?

Page 27 – Fill in the blank:
- Fear

Week 4: Who is God? – Part 2

Page 29 – Fill in the blanks:
- Carries
- Forget
- Comforts
- Great delight
- Gifts
- Gathers

Week 6: Our Need for Love and Approval

Pages 35, 36 – Fill in the blanks:
- "Behold a son" – giving birth to a son was a great honor in that society
- "God hears"
- "Companion"

- "Let Him (God) be praised"
- "To hire"
- "Dwelling"

Week 7: Loss and Grief
Pages 37, 38 – Fill in the blanks:
- Working
- Healthy
- Time and work

Week 8: What Does Your Past Look Like?
Page 41 – Fill in the blanks:
- Righteous
- Devalues

Page 43 – Fill in the blank:
- Followed God

Page 44 –
When God speaks to us through His Word, a dream, a thought in our hearts or another person, it will agree with what the Bible teaches. We will also have a strong feeling of peace. Other people may confirm what we are sensing from God.

Week 9: Secrets to Defeating Sins
Page 48 – We can use God's Word to change our thought patterns. To do this we must:
- Read the Bible
- Meditate on what it says
- Journal on what you feel God is saying to you
- Make a plan for applying these truths
- Be accountable to someone you trust

Week 10: Our Confidence
Page 54 –
1. Love
2. Knowledge
3. Deep insight

Week 11: Who Am I?
Page 57 – Fill in the blanks:
- Spirit
- Purpose

Week 12: Truth or Lies?
Page 61 – Does Jesus care?

Jesus responded to their cries even as they questioned His love for them. He may have been testing their faith. He was definitely helping them to grow in faith!

How we see ourselves is crucial to how we trust God. Sometimes we get stuck on the same old views. It is time to see ourselves as God sees us and move forward in our pursuit of Him.

Week 13: Freedom from Anger
Pages 66, 67 – Fill in the blanks
- Emotion

Steps to freedom:
1. Cause
2. Facts
3. Responsibility
4. Eyes
5. Opportunity
6. Quickly
7. Surrendered
8. Offenders
9. Benefits
10. Personal rights
11. Accountable
12. Filled

Week 14: Caring for One Another
Page 69 – Fill in the blank:
- Action

Week 15: Pain and Shame
Tamar was beautiful and innocent. When David told her to go to see Amnon, she had no choice. She begged him not to do it.

Week 17: Dealing with Negative Words
Nehemiah's enemies tried to block his success because they hated the Jews and wanted to be in control.

Week 18: Healthy Confrontation
Page 77 – Fill in the blanks:
1. Issues
2. Yourself, motives
3. Person
4. Kind

Week 22: Boundaries
Page 86 - Fill in the blank:
- Presence

ABOUT THE AUTHOR

Laverne Weber is an ordained minister with a specific calling and God-given ability to reach those who are hurting. She is also a nurse, teacher, and speaker who delivers life-changing truth filled with compassion and humor. She received her calling into the Lord's service as a missionary child in Sierra Leone, West Africa.

In 1993, Laverne founded *Victory's Journey™ Ministries*, formerly Journey to Joy, a ministry for those who are broken. She also serves with her husband as part-time pastors at Faith Community Assembly of God in Easton. The Webers have three children and four grandchildren.

It is one of her greatest joys to see the Holy Spirit set God's children free to grow into His purpose for them.

www.ingramcontent.com/pod-product-compliance
Lightning Source LLC
LaVergne TN
LVHW061248060426
835508LV00018B/1550